LOVED BACK TO LIFE

Healing isn't Just Possible, It's Promised;
A True Story of Trauma, Faith, and
Redeeming Love

TORI HARRISON

Copyright © 2025 *Tori Harrison*

Published by CaryPress International Books

www.CaryPress.com

All rights reserved. No part of this publication may be reproduced, distributed, or transmitted in any form or by any means, including photocopying, recording, or other electronic or mechanical methods, without the prior written permission of the publisher, except in the case of brief quotations embodied in critical reviews and certain other non-commercial uses permitted by copyright law.

Table of Contents

Foreword	*vii*
Trauma: A Deeply Distressing or Disturbing Experience	*xi*
It Starts Small	1
Estrangement and the Beginning of the Telenovela	7
Rehab and a Wolf in Sheep's Clothing	11
Can Anyone Hear Me?	15
God's plan? Wasn't interested.	19
Am I Thin Enough Yet?	23
Sowing Good Seeds	27
Finally, Someone Else Gets It + Cups of Crazy	33
A Slow Re-Entrance Back Into Real Life, Purity, and a Relapse	39
Childlike Joy and Stripping Away My Old Self	45
The Cindy Saga Continues	49
Searching for "Home"	53
Juvie and the Presence of the Lord	59
Out with the Old, In with the New: Another Stepping Stone to Jesus	65
No Roots	71

Nomad Life + A Christmas Revelation	73
My Buddy the Box, It Gets Worse Before It Gets Better	79
Making Emancipation Official	87
Wild + Free, Homeless Summer	91
A Loving Intervention + Summer's Dramatic Close	97
A Strange Scheme	101
Texas + A Double Life	107
Sin Will Take You Further Than You Ever Thought You Could Go	111
Plot Twist	117
Sitting in the Trauma + Why It's Imperative to Healing	121
Stacking Distractions + a Lesson in Who You Allow Close	125
People Can't Fill The Voids That Only Jesus Can	129
What's The Fruit?	133
God's Patience and Goodbyes	135
Helloooo Ohio + Going All In	139
All Things Revealed	145
Learning to Fly on my Own	151
No More Running, No More Forcing	155
God Can Change Your Entire Life in 24 hours + Walking in Obedience	157
Self-Sufficiency + What Real Love Looks Like	159

A New 'Step Mom' + A Side of Karma	165
People are Not Your Enemy, the Enemy himself is	169
Church Hurt – We All Got It + We're All Sinners In Need Of Grace	173
Peace out, Party girl; Marriage + Another Step Towards Healing	177
Our Wedding, Boundaries + An Attempt For Reconciliation	183
Seventy-Seven Times – The Opposite of Society	189
You, Again?	193
God Provides Mentors + Mother Figures	197
The Ultimate Parent, Provider, and Best Friend	201
God Takes Marriage Seriously and So Should We	205
We Have a Choice To Heal	209
The Way We Use Our Voice + Set Boundaries	213
Turning Over a New Leaf	217
The Gift of Time	221
Doing Our Part in Healing – Apologies + Hard Conversations	223
Keeping It Real + Being Exactly Who God Created You to Be	227
Breaking Off Generation Cycles	231
It Gets Better	233
Self Awareness + Facing the Trauma	237

Foreword

There are stories that whisper, and there are stories that roar. Tori Harrison's story roars with the kind of truth that cuts through pretense and reaches straight into the soul. In a world that often asks us to curate our pain into palatable soundbites, Tori offers something radical: unflinching honesty about the messy, heartbreaking, and ultimately redemptive journey from trauma to healing.

This isn't a fairy tale. It's not a neat narrative where everything gets tied up with a bow. It's real life—the kind that leaves scars, teaches hard lessons, and ultimately reveals the extraordinary grace that can emerge from the most broken places. Tori takes us into the raw reality of family dysfunction, addiction, homelessness, and abandonment—not to shock or sensationalize, but to illuminate the path from darkness to light that so many of us desperately need to see.

What makes this memoir extraordinary isn't just Tori's courage to tell her story; it's her wisdom in understanding that our deepest wounds can become our greatest sources of strength. She doesn't minimize the pain or rush to the happy ending. Instead, she shows us how God meets us in the middle of our mess, how healing happens not in spite of our brokenness but often because of it.

As you read these pages, you'll find yourself laughing at Tori's self-deprecating humor, crying at the depth of hurt she endured, and cheering for the young woman who refused to let her circumstances define her destiny. You'll also find something perhaps even more valuable: practical wisdom for your own journey. Tori doesn't just tell us what happened; she shares what she learned, how she grew, and how the same God who met her in juvenile detention centers and rehab facilities is ready to meet you wherever you are.

This book is for anyone who has ever felt abandoned, misunderstood, or written off. It's for those who carry invisible wounds from family trauma, who struggle with the weight of expectations they can never meet, or who wonder if their story matters. Tori's journey from a hurting teenager with a cardboard box of belongings to a healed woman who breaks generational cycles is proof that no one is too broken, too far gone, or too messed up for redemption.

Loved Back to Life is ultimately about exactly what the title promises—being loved back to life by a God who pursues us relentlessly, who sees beauty in our ashes, and who specializes in making all things new. It's about learning that healing isn't just possible; it's promised. And sometimes, the very experiences that nearly destroy us become the foundation for the life we were always meant to live.

Prepare to be moved, challenged, and ultimately hopeful. Tori's story will remind you that no matter what your beginning looked like, God isn't finished writing your story yet.

~Ana Starns, Ph. D.
Memoir Therapy

Trauma: A Deeply Distressing or Disturbing Experience

as defined by the good old dictionary

We all have *some* trauma. Some may have had one or two events that affected them, while others have had a series of significant traumas that completely shaped them as human beings. I'm in the latter bracket, myself. Whether we decide to face those traumas head-on and heal from them is up to us.

When I was a little girl, I thought life was fairy dust and sparkles, and we ate cake every day. I always exploded with joy. I look back and think how sunny and goofy my disposition naturally was – who I *really* was, and am, at my core. Doesn't that sound like a good time? Honestly, now at 30, I'm the closest I've ever been to that pure joy I had as a little babe again because of the love, healing, and peace Jesus has given me. God has that joy for you, too, if you'll grab hold of it and hang on tight. It took years to get to this place – years of sifting through traumas and destructive behaviors and switching from the mindset of "How could this happen to me?" to "How is God going to use this?" If you're asking yourself the first question more so than the second, I'm here to tell you that *it gets better* and there is a purpose that can come from your experiences and pain!

In the pages of this book, I'll share with you the personal stories that shaped my trauma: how God repeatedly pursued me through drug use, homelessness, and unfortunate family circumstances. I'll take you on my journey of how He healed me from every traumatic experience, covered me in grace, and why I finally chose an abundant life in Him.

It Starts Small

I remember when things started to go south in my parents' marriage when I was around seven years old, but I distinctly remember a moment when I recognized that it was getting worse at age twelve. I was sitting in church next to both my parents, and the pastor proclaimed, "There's a demonic spirit in one of the women here!" My mom told me later that my dad had whispered to her that it was her. Whether or not that's the real reason we never sat in those pews again is still a mystery, but the fact that we didn't changed my life. Isn't it wild how we can remember a seemingly small pivotal moment that changed the course of our lives? I had no idea at the time that it was just the beginning.

That church was all I really knew. A cozy, welcoming, safe-haven where everyone was *literally* family – or at least about fifty percent of them were my relatives. Leaving that church felt like someone had shaken me awake, and my eyes were opened, as if someone had popped my little bubble. At home, I became hyper-focused on my parents' little arguments that would escalate in minutes and force me to choose sides. Even around seven and eight years old, I have memories of being asked, "Who do you think is right, Tori?"

After an argument, I would be pulled in two directions as each tried to get me to take their side. I would usually end up with my mom on a vengeful shopping trip. What little girl wouldn't choose that? I was just a kid! That was like giving me the option between cake or vegetables. Go shopping for pretty things with Mom or go to the movie store with Dad…check yes to shopping. I didn't fully understand at such a young age what was really going on between the two of them or that I was being used as a chess piece. Maybe they weren't aware of what they were doing, but that's what was happening. As tension grew between my parents, I grew more hyper-aware, overwhelmed, and angry. I felt like I was swirled into their hostility towards one another and forced to play monkey in the middle or referee. Ultimately, it became a game of leverage and who had me on their side; they didn't want to hear how I felt about any of it. My perception is that since they had no control over their marriage or each other, they tried to control me. I was made to feel like I had no voice. Not being allowed to have a voice made me run from any poke that made me feel the slightest bit manipulated or pushed to the side. Eventually, this became a pattern that led me down a path of addiction and running from anything that caused me pain.

I felt as though a looming beast was about to be unleashed after my brothers left home, as if it was one of those 'keep it together until the kids leave' moments. However, I was still there, and I was still very young; I wasn't leaving anytime soon. There was a tense feeling of the question, "Now what do we do with the last kid?"

I have always been intuitive, discerning, and attentive to everything going on around me, and I felt things deeply, even as a kid. As tension grew between my parents, I grew more hyper aware, overwhelmed, and angry. I felt like I was swirled into their hostility towards one another and forced to play monkey in the middle or referee. Ultimately, it became a game of leverage and who had me on their side; they didn't want to hear how I felt about any of it. My perception is that since they had no control of their marriage or each other, they tried to control me. I was made to feel like I had no voice. Not being allowed to have a voice made me run from any poke that made me feel the slightest bit manipulated or pushed to the side. Eventually, this became a pattern that led me down a path of addiction and running from anything that caused me pain. I wasn't really taught boundaries as a kid because my parents were so involved in their own world, and I always felt like my needs and questions were too much of a burden to add to their fire. The lack of boundaries just led to more of a deep dive into self-medicating and running away, both physically and emotionally. Ya girl was running a marathon!

At thirteen, I got in with a crowd that I had no business hanging with; they were all at least five to ten years older than I was. Cigarettes and drunken nights in parking lots or around bonfires became an escape and fed the addiction monster, exacerbating the pattern of running away from any inkling of emotional pain. Isn't it crazy how the enemy will orchestrate the perfect mess, and it ends up setting your entire life on fire?

The people who bought me cigarettes and alcohol were the same people I resonated with and who I felt most loved by – we became a messy little family. I can look back now and see God's word come to life in those moments - "And we know that for those who love God all things work together for good, for those who are called according to His purpose" (Romans 8:28). Those people were in the same boat I was, but in different ways. We had all bonded over trauma, and because of this, we all treasured our relationships with each other more. Our friendship was a haven for all of us; the problem was that we were all self-medicating with each other, too. We were out there, unintentionally trauma bonding! The enemy is so slick in using something well-intentioned in a negative way, but God graced me with those people so that I would feel seen and understood. He flipped it for the good.

I have only recently learned what my mom's childhood was like and what her mom, who died before I was born, was like. My grandma had all the jokes, had nicknames for everything, and was just a good time to be around. So many goofy things about her explain parts of who I am. I really wish I could have experienced who she was! My mom's sister, my aunt, has shared a lot that has answered many questions I've had for years, but I still can't wrap my head around why my mom never shared any details of her childhood or her own mother with me. I wonder if she experienced traumas that were too painful for her to talk about. I'm not sure I'll ever know her experiences from her own mouth, but I am so grateful to her sister for helping me understand her past a little bit more. Sometimes, in order to heal from our traumas, we need the backstory about the people who caused them.

Estrangement and the Beginning of the Telenovela

There don't seem to be many self-help books or cure-all spiritual advice about grieving the death of someone who is still alive. I've had to do this twice – with my mom and my brother. I've found that people straight up don't talk about estrangement from family, although it's everywhere, especially in today's "cancel culture." So many people have and still act like it didn't happen, or even weirder, like those people just don't exist anymore, making the whole thing confusing and difficult to navigate.

Well, my friend, if you're sitting in this weird grief box, I'm here to sit with you and hopefully make you feel less alone. Time does heal – our older and wiser grandparents aren't wrong. Let me explain…and before you begin to think, "Um, so far this is very soap-opera-TV-drama-series feeling," Yes, it is, and it was – but it's all real. You could say it was a real-life telenovela.

Shortly after we had left the family church I'd grown up in, we ended up at a massive church that felt contrived. It almost felt like a concert performance in comparison to the hymnals and small congregation of about eighty people I was accustomed to. It was a whole new world! During that time, my mom made a new friend, Cindy. This 'best friend' became the wrench thrown in that caused our whole family to rattle, and what deteriorated my relationship with my mom. I think since my mom lost her mother so young, she was seeking an older woman to walk through life with her. I don't blame her one bit for that aspect, but she made unfortunate decisions that were influenced by Cindy that led to the loss of her own family over the next five years.

I remember Cindy coming around every so often when I was 13, but as I got older, she was at our house every time I turned around. Red flags started to wave for me when I was in high school. I quickly noticed how odd the friendship was between her and my mom. It mimicked a mother-daughter relationship, but stranger. My mom was no longer present with her family and became more invested in the relationship with Cindy, as though she was making up for lost time with someone she thought could take the place of her mother. I remember overhearing Cindy scolding my mom in the kitchen like an older parent would and thinking how weird it was that her 'friend' would talk to her like that. I knew something was wildly off.

Not long after that incident, accusations started rolling in from Cindy about every member of my family. These weren't your average accusations, though; I'm talking weird, "What on God's green earth would make you believe a thing like that?" accusations. It was so puzzling to me because the Mom I knew before Cindy wouldn't stand for someone disrespecting her family with such outrageously false claims. Once, my mom told me Cindy had called her to tell her that my brother (who lived in California at the time) was sitting on her bed with a gun when she got home. The story was outrageous, but the most insane part of it all was that my Mom believed her wholeheartedly. I tried to explain to her that it's not humanly possible for someone to be in two places at once, nevermind the fact that my brother wouldn't buy a plane ticket to come and sit on the bed of some woman he's barely met, but to do so with a gun in his hands for no reason. These types of accusations poured in on a weekly basis: off-the-wall stories that had no rhyme or reason to them, stories that any normal person would have been like, "Hold on, you're making accusations and talking crazy about my family, and that's a no for me." For no logical reason I could see, other than the obvious spiritual and mental confusion that was unfolding, my mom held onto every false spun story this woman fed her.

As time went on, my mom seemed to slowly lose her grip on reality. I remember at 16, I was temporarily living with a friend, and I called my mom from my friend's cell since I didn't have one. I thought she might have wanted to know if I was doing ok, though I wasn't going to tell her where I was because I couldn't trust her. My mom emphatically accused me of drinking at a bonfire at that very moment. I looked around me, sitting in my friend's breezeway.

"Uh…are you ok?" I asked. "I'm looking at a blueberry field right now."

She snapped back, "Cindy said that you're with an old boyfriend right now around a bonfire, drinking, and she can see you!"

I laughed and retorted, "Well, hate to break it to you, but that's not where I am because it's not possible."

She asked when I would "stop lying," then hung up.

There were so many instances like this that continued throughout those five years that I was treating the house as a revolving door. My mother had convinced every family member that I was the wayward daughter, based on what Cindy had told her. I felt helpless and like no one would listen to me because, unfortunately, my mom was excellent at spinning the stories, and I was out self-medicating, which didn't look good to everyone else. I didn't hide that I was self-medicating. It's like I was sitting in a sinking boat with a sign that said, "Help!" and both of my parents knew, but didn't seem to know how to spend time on me to prevent the boat from sinking further. In many ways, the world was my teacher, similar to the mean teacher who always flunked you because they didn't like you! The devil was busy.

Rehab and a Wolf in Sheep's Clothing

Let's flip it in reverse for a second. This seems like the perfect spot to share the rehab saga of my life. Did you just sing Amy Winehouse, too? Somehow, rehab became my parents' Band-Aid for me throughout my teenage years. When they found cigarettes in my bag at thirteen, my mom lied to me and said that we were going to Grand Rapids to go shopping, but she took me to an outpatient facility instead. I'll never forget the counselor looking at both of us, perplexed, and asking, "Your daughter has a pack of cigarettes, so you brought her here? Why? Why are you really here?" My mom replied, pointing at me frantically, "So you can help her!"

I can look back on this now and laugh. This was the first of three rehabilitation centers I was forced to go to. Somehow, she always left with the same conclusion – that everything was my fault and I needed to be "fixed." If someone could just "fix" me, it would all get better for her! No shocker here that after one week of intense all-day counseling, I was not fixed and did not leave with a signed paper and gold star that said "perfect child." I don't say any of this with a condescending or disrespectful intention – I can laugh and see it plainly as an attack from Satan on who I was, even as a young girl.

There was nothing "wrong" with me. I was a thirteen-year-old who needed love, time, and most importantly, a mother who wasn't being manipulated by a woman whose clear intention (to me) was to destroy our relationship. Ultimately, Cindy's mission was to destroy our family and cut my mom off from everyone she knew. That's all I had understood at that time, but I didn't understand *why*. It became somewhat of a never-ending murder mystery dinner, except no one *actually* died; they just got removed from my mom's life. I used to wonder if Cindy had a checklist she was going down or a corkboard in her basement with what her next move would be to completely destroy my mom. In hindsight, I see it was all calculated. *But why?! What reason did she have to target my mom and our family?* Slowly, Mom's relationships with friends started ending, followed by family. Cindy had a seemingly personal agenda against my Mom, without reason.

Since the beginning of time, the enemy has had an extra malicious agenda toward women. Think about it: we give birth to *life!* In the Garden of Eden, the serpent preyed on Eve's vulnerability and kindness, her eagerness to invite and trust. We nurture, we love hard, and we have empathy, grace, and mercy. We have a beautiful softness to us that the enemy preys on and manipulates through various ways in this world. God made us special as women.

Sometimes, it *will feel more challenging and unfair as a woman in this world*. But the fight is worth it. I wish another woman had bestowed that truth on me when I was younger. I saw the enemy and the unfortunate work of his hands deep within my mom's life as he slowly tore our family apart. On the flip side, God patched it back together in His uniquely perfect way, as you'll read as my testimony continues to unfold within the pages of this book.

Throughout the next year, things slid downhill even further between my parents and I. Cindy continued to spew untrue stories about me and my family like it was her job, and I grew to feel more helpless and neglected. No one would listen to me when I spoke, so I decided to do something about it, which seemed very logical to my thirteen-year-old brain. Remember years ago when cutting seemed to be a big topic of conversation? Unfortunately, it was happening a lot. There were a lot of reasons kids were doing it; although my reasoning was out of pain. I felt numb, like I wasn't heard or seen. I'll admit that part of my intent was that if my parents found out, they would care and ask me why. I would then have been able to explain everything, and they would have seen what they were doing – what Cindy was causing – and we would sing "Kumbaya" while hugging. They noticed my arm was slashed, and after a brief conversation that mostly consisted of my mom being angry with me, she decided intense counseling at a rehab center would, again, be the solution. The counselor spoke to my mom first, which changed the perspective of the counselor. That resulted in a horrendous experience of taking sleeping medications that didn't work in the process of trying to, once again, "fix" me. Somehow, the conclusion was that the so-called "behavioral issues" that I was having were because of a lack of sleep. *What?* I know; I still can't figure that one out.

I want to be clear, it wasn't *only* my parents' decisions that led to some rough roads and poor life choices. I now know that it was due to massive issues with my home life, my need for adventure, and some teenage hormones thrown into the mix. I truly thought I was grown and knew it all at thirteen. You couldn't tell me a dang thing! With how much hardship I had already encountered, I thought I'd seen it all. Pair that with sky-high confidence and already being somewhat of an old soul at such a young age, it didn't help that I looked at least nineteen and was well aware of it. I didn't blink when I saw a cop with a cigarette in my hand. I knew I looked old enough, and they almost never questioned me. I didn't think anyone cared what I did because no one would listen to me anyway, so I became enamored with taking risks. I always thought that I was untouchable, with no grasp of what real repercussions looked like, until I finally did get caught.

Can Anyone Hear Me?

The first time I got caught stealing was at thirteen. The judge put me on probation for nine months, along with community service. None of it fazed me, and I continued stealing from stores without any remorse. I would have never stolen from anyone's home, but for some reason, stealing what I wanted from different stores gave me a sense of control. Is that backwards? Yes. But pain and trauma can come out in ways we don't understand until later on. Not long after my probation, I was charged with an MIP (Minor in Possession) for smoking cigarettes outside of a coffee shop. A week or so after that, I had another court date where my probation was extended by an extra six months. You would think that would shake me a little bit, but I was so very, very numb. Unfortunately, that was the first of many court dates, drug charges, probation sentences, driving tickets, traffic violations, and court-mandated classes. We can all facepalm together!

Throughout this time, nothing had improved at home. By fourteen, the amount of crazy that had unfolded in my first year of teenagehood was enough for ten years. I was tired. It was strange to me that my parents didn't ask questions or say anything, given how much was happening. I know that little girl in me desperately wanted my parents to take notice and genuinely care about what was going on, to take the time to show me love. I longed for them to simply listen and really hear what I was feeling. I had expectations put on me to fit a Perfect Polly Box that I could not meet, but they could not see any fault in their actions, especially my mom, and I was boxed into a corner. At that point, the only thing I could think to do was to take my own life.

Mom left for work one afternoon, and things were bad enough that I felt like it was easier on me and everyone else to take my own life. I scrambled through the medicine cabinet in the kitchen, reaching for anything I could find. After downing most of a bottle of sleeping pills, I was immediately filled with remorse. I didn't really want to die; I wanted someone to see me, for my voice to be heard. I grabbed the phone to call my best friend at the time and told her what I had done, and thankfully, she called 911. All I remember is waking up in the hospital the next morning, my mom sitting next to me. Instead of trying to understand or ask me why I'd done it, she was furious, which was the worst thing she could have done in that moment after such a tremendous cry for help. I felt helpless and hopeless in every way as the hospital sent me off to rehab again in an ambulance in the hope that someone else would "fix me" and return me as the version of me they'd been hoping for.

This time, rehab was a horrifying experience, being an inpatient for a week instead of an outpatient. My roommate had an extreme case of bipolar disorder, which was my first experience trying to understand what bipolar even was. The girl across the hall from me tried to kill her parents with a kitchen knife and was strangely monotone in describing it to me with an obvious lack of remorse. The guy in our support group was an extreme pyro-maniac, and the little four-year-old girl in the padded room down the hall spent the majority of her time running in circles, screaming. She had some other mental health issues and was hallucinating that the Seed of Chucky was chasing her due to her parents allowing her to watch the movie repeatedly (yes, for real!). I can't make this stuff up!

To say the least, I was extremely out of place. I knew I wasn't a bad kid, just very misunderstood and lacking love, care, or support. I was discharged a week later, and as soon as I got in the car, my dad turned to ask me, "Do you feel better now?" To prevent him from thinking I wasn't fixed enough for fear of him putting me back in rehab, I replied with an exhausted "Sure" under my breath. Truthfully, I felt worse and more patronized than before I went in. The experience of that week scarred me and messed with my head in ways I could never have explained. I realized I could never get my parents to love me the way I needed them to.

To move forward, I knew I had to sever myself from them emotionally, mentally, and physically in order to survive. I went into self-preservation mode, somewhere between fight or flight at all times. On the car ride home that day, I think something inside of me switched. I decided I was going to fight for myself, which was a great thing! I began a new journey on my own, to try and figure out how to live a happy life in safety without my parents, at fourteen. Little did I know, it would be a *long*, hellish fight for five more years.

God's plan? Wasn't interested.

Sometimes it's hard for me to keep the timeline of my life in order because there was such a painful amount of traumatic events that unfolded in a very short time span. I have to rack my brain for what happened next, how it happened, and if it came before this or that. When high school started, my parents thought the best decision was to put me in a private Baptist Christian school. I was a very loud, angry, and relatively jaded girl by then. I had no interest in God's plan for my life, as I didn't understand why He would allow the events in my life to unfold the way they had.

The school was small, and when I say small, I mean the graduating class was three people. It was a tiny school inside of a church, with a small classroom wing that resembled the elementary school wing I went to as a child. There was a mandatory Bible class, which was excruciating for me to walk into each week because of my anger towards God. I hated the school for being based on the Bible, the people for how inauthentic they seemed, and I made it very clear to everyone that I didn't want to be there – especially my parents.

I believe that even at that time, God was planting seeds for me, though. I still remember learning about the Father, Son, and Holy Spirit in an approachable way. It also woke me up to the difference between religious people and spirit-filled people. In that space, God started to define my gifts and open my eyes. Some of those things I wouldn't recognize until years later. God was gently unwinding me.

My grades throughout my high school career were the absolute least important thing to me – people took precedence. Relationships and having fun were always number one! I thought that there was so much life meant to be lived and I wasn't going to waste it learning crap I wouldn't utilize later. I wish I had had a little more balance in that. When my grades plummeted and a meeting was called, I took my opportunity to let them know how I felt about their school. I didn't have much of a filter back then as a result of being deeply hurt, so if I didn't like you, it was literally like unleashing the kraken. I didn't take any ounce of crap from people.

The meeting was short and sweet, really. I think they were hoping that I would want to leave, and I was more than happy to do so. With that door slammed, I was off to the big high school in town for the remainder of my freshman year! I was so stoked to have a normal social life and I had high hopes that things would look up for me, being in a less-constrained environment. Boy, was I wrong! It was only a bigger pool for me to play in. There was so much more at my fingertips! I started dabbling with prescription drugs and getting high off of whatever I could possibly get my hands on. I was mentally running, and when nothing would suffice, I would try mixing things or find something new. At some point, I developed a philosophy (which I now know without a doubt was the enemy's doing), that I needed to "open my mind" and try every drug. I was searching for anything and everything but God to fill the void inside of me. At school, I was collecting detentions like Pokémon cards from no shows and tardies, and that eventually got me a one-on-one meeting with the school director and a warning: if I didn't start trying with my grades, they'd have to expel me. That didn't faze me. To me, there was still no interest from anyone to ask what the root of the problem was. And if they had asked, there would have been too much to tell. I was also accustomed to adults not listening and being unsafe, so why would I have told them anything? It seemed like a waste of my time.

It couldn't have been more than a month later that I was suspended. I was so hopped up on pills in my classes, one of the teachers had started to take notice and took me outside of the classroom to ask me what was going on. I brushed her off and tried to act as sober as possible, but my pupils must have been the size of UFOs. I was also selling various pills at the time, and someone mentioned it to the principal, which landed me in his office. The police officer searched me, finding a few pills in my jacket. They called my dad, who was angry but didn't seem to be surprised; both of my parents were understandably tired of me getting into trouble at school. I knew it was only a matter of time before something was going to happen, they weren't going to keep putting up with me pushing the envelope. In part, I think my goal was to push it just far enough that they would look up from themselves and see that I simply needed them to invest in me, unconditionally.

Underneath it all, I sought their love and attention, like any kid at that age.

Am I Thin Enough Yet?

One of the best things I've discovered over the years is that no one views hurt the same way as me – we all view incidents in different ways, and we all internalize trauma differently. A lot more people than I thought have a trauma response of completely blocking events out of their memory altogether; however, their body still remembers, and eventually it comes out in other ways. It's common to see it result in addiction or erratic behaviors. Most of the time, they don't know or can't explain why they act like that, because they need help getting to the root of where it's coming from. Some people weren't taught how to process or verbalize trauma, and some were taught they weren't allowed to express when they're hurt by someone else at all. Bottling and stuffing hurts *you,* not the other person. If we don't share what's hurt us, someone may never know or understand, and we can't expect people to read our minds! Almost no one thinks the same way we do. Although it may never "click" for them, when we express that they've hurt us, acknowledgement and an apology is a non-negotiable to having a healthy relationship!

For most of my childhood, I was a chunky little girl. I would receive a lot of comments from my brothers, and many times even my dad about my weight. When I was around five, my brother took me in the kitchen, got a knife out of the drawer, and said, "Your fat could all be gone! This is all you have to do!" Thankfully, my mom walked in and scolded him. I'm sure he was joking, but it stayed with me forever and affected me more than he could have foreseen at that moment. Since then, I've brought up how that affected me, and he's apologized for the hurt that was ingrained from that incident.

Without consulting me, my parents hired a weekly personal trainer when I was in the ninth grade. After two meetings, I told them that I could lose the weight on my own. In the back of my mind, I wondered if that was why they didn't pay much attention to me. I thought to myself, "Is this really it? Do I just need to be a certain weight to catch their attention?" How sad that I felt like that; it breaks my heart for teenage me! At that time, I was thirty pounds overweight from depressive overeating, and I *did* need to lose weight, but I wasn't losing weight for health reasons – I was losing weight to gain my parents' attention, so it jump-started a skewed relationship with food and my body. To lose the weight, I went in headfirst with zero chill: I began running on the treadmill, eating little to nothing every day – only about five hundred calories. When I put my mind to something, I am dedicated to it, but to my detriment this time. A little over a month later, over thirty pounds were gone, but I had gained an unhealthy obsession with losing weight. I was seeking approval from family after being teased for my weight, all while hoping it was the thing that would finally get my parents to pay more attention to me.

There were a few times when I had passed out at home and at school from a lack of food. I remember being in the hospital after passing out once, unsure of how I got there, and the doctor told me my kidneys weren't functioning properly, and if I didn't start eating, I was going to die. I was *so* hardheaded then–that news still wasn't enough to shake me! I actually remember thinking that it couldn't be true. I felt that I still had weight to lose, and the doctor was just trying to get me to eat by scaring me. I had developed such body dysmorphia that it rolled into a lie that I could never be thin enough. With the issues at school and home piling up, my parents didn't know what to do. The only thing they knew to resort to, once again, was to put me in rehab.

Sowing Good Seeds

After an hour of Saturday detention at school, my parents picked me up and told me we were going "Christmas shopping." I knew this trick all too well – Mom had done it the first time she coerced me into going to rehab. When we pulled into a Denny's parking lot, I felt my stomach drop. I immediately had an intuition that this time would be more serious. First, my mom was a health nut, so I don't think I had ever seen the inside of a Denny's in my entire life! And secondly, the drive there was *not* filled with holiday cheer or Christmas music; it was silent and uncomfortable. My parents were glancing at one another, so I had a feeling that something was going on. Sure enough, as soon as I stepped out of the car, Scott, who I would soon find out was the director of the rehab facility, was walking towards me. I knew exactly what was going on. He asked me if I'd been "Having trouble at home," to which I quickly replied, "No." I was ready to run in any direction to get away from the inevitable. He said, "We can do this the easy way or the hard way," and let me tell you, if you ever looked at this six-foot-something man with a white van behind him that looked like one of those creepy serial killer vans…you would freeze dead in your tracks, too! Disappointed but not surprised, I watched my parents pull a pre-packed suitcase out of the back of the car. They went in for a quick hug, but I turned away and got into the van. I knew the rehab drill by then; I just wondered how long it would be this time.

When we first pulled into the driveway of Pathway of Hope, an in-home facility for girls in the Middle of Nowhere, Michigan, I had a feeling in the pit of my stomach that this time would be different. I just didn't realize that I was pulling into one of the biggest journeys of my life! I walked into the room where there were about ten girls staring at me. All of these girls were from wildly different backgrounds, and each of them already had big testimonies at such young ages, like myself. I met the two girls who would be my roommates, who, thankfully, welcomed me immediately.

Ashley was severely bipolar, and I was slightly afraid of her. Sam was transferred from the jail and had a three-year-old girl, Molly. I became close with Sam right away. She had already been there for about two years. She was quiet, and I could tell she was exhausted, waiting for what was next for her and her daughter, hoping for someone to adopt them.

The first night that I arrived, we were all required to go to the local church. I broke down in a river of tears during worship. Angry at God, I wept quietly in disbelief that this had happened yet again. Why can't my parents see that they're the issue? Why does this keep happening? I wondered if I would ever have stability or a normal life. What did a normal life even look like? I had no clue at that time. The next morning, one of the counselors gave me a book about eating disorders that I was forced to read as the beginning of my therapy. I began to feel a little safer when she looked me in the eyes and said, "Tori, we genuinely love you. I know this is scary, but things will get better, and you're surrounded by people who love you. This is a safe place..." There was something about her honesty that made me believe her. For the first time ever, I felt *heard* as she listened to *my* side of the story.

Spending Christmas with a short hour-long visitation with all of our parents at the local church was so hard; they may as well have just let us have a ten-minute phone call. We were all lined up in chairs and had opened our presents, which were the same for all of us. Some basic needs items mostly, then we quickly said goodbye to our parents. Though I've tried to forget it, it's been seared into my brain that it didn't feel like Christmas at all.

Sharing a room with Ashley, who had hallucinations in the middle of the night, was terrifying. It's a graphic thing to imagine, but I distinctly remember an episode she had one night when she hallucinated that she was killing her brother. The night staff came in and told Sam and me not to move. Some of the things I experienced throughout my stints in rehab revealed a new form of empathy for people. A few months into being there, Sam and her daughter were transferred to Kids First, a transitional home for families. This happened pretty often, girls coming in and out over a few months, and we would never find out why. I was so sad to see her go, but thrilled for her that she was on her way to establishing a good life!

There were cameras in all of the rooms, with three girls per room. It was strange…it was a comfortable house, but with a feeling of being in jail every day, between the cameras always watching and the very strict regimen we all followed. There were Levels as part of the program, and we had to work our way up to Level Four to graduate from the program. Different colors indicated the different Levels; whichever Level we were on was the color of the t-shirt we had to wear every day. Plain colored Hanes t-shirts are all I wore for about three months until I got to the Level where I was allowed to wear my own clothes again (hallelujah!). Yellow shirts meant we were in trouble and had to sit at the table in solitude until they said we were done being punished. The staff gave each girl a number to keep track of our belongings, I was number five, so I had to number all of my clothes and items in permanent marker on the tags. It's been wild finding little fives written in some clothes I haven't yet gotten rid of over the years!

They were pretty transparent about funding with us there. There wasn't a lot of money to fund the program; they only received a certain amount of money from the state every month. It wasn't enough for as many girls as were there, so unfortunately we ate like crap – a lot of junk and bulk foods. I put on weight faster than I had ever thought possible, and it crushed me to not have the option of making healthy food choices, as that was something that would have made me feel good, both mentally and physically. What was offered was what you got, or you didn't eat. That really forced me to face my issues with food and body image through counseling there head-on.

We were required to attend the local church every Sunday, and most Wednesdays, too. Honestly, the more I grew in my relationship with God and worked through my anger with Him, was incredible how my view of myself changed. Jesus completely flipped the lens, and I began to have confidence, seeing myself as He saw me. It was assuredness in *who* I am rather than *what* I am. My identity started to shift from what I looked like, what I'd done, what my circumstances were, to who Jesus says I am!

"But you are a chosen people, a royal priesthood, a holy nation, God's special possession, that you may declare the praises of Him who called you out of darkness into his wonderful light" (1 Peter 2:9).

Finally, Someone Else Gets It + Cups of Crazy

We started having family counseling sessions about two months into my stay, and my word, they were brutal. There was a lot of harbored anger, not just towards me, but between my parents, which in many ways had been taken out on me. They required my parents to start making an extra trip to the facility every month for separate marriage counseling sessions. Frankly, I knew from what one of the staff told me in a meeting that they saw what I saw and knew that, because of their marital problems, I had suffered from similar issues. Hearing that was like someone telling you you're not crazy! It was the reassurance I needed. The staff became family and were very protective, which was healing for me, especially from the women on staff who had become like big sisters and mamas to me. It was healing the places in me that had begun to despise women because of the way I'd been treated by my mom.

I remember one particular counseling session where Mom looked at Dad and tearfully said she hated him. For some reason, it really rocked me because it was what I had already felt between them, but now that it was said out loud, it was real. I had also never seen them be that honest with one another. Like any kid, I didn't want to hear that my parents' relationship was in that place, even though I already knew it was. They continued those sessions until I graduated from the program five months later. The counselors themselves told me that through those sessions, my parents' marriage was saved (temporarily, but we'll get to that later). I was happy for them, but I was also irate that I had to suffer in rehab again for them to figure out that they were a large part of the problem. I know that God placed me there for personal development as well, but dang! It was such a prime example in hindsight that God works out ALL things for our good and His glory (Romans 8:28). Jesus brought evvvverything full circle in that season! There were so many small victories of healing for the three of us in those counseling rooms, and for that, I'm grateful.

I got a new bunkmate–who we'll call something wild because that was very much her personality - Candie! Our new roommate was a fourteen-year-old self-proclaimed cocaine dealer transferred from juvie. I think what we all had in common at Pathway was that we were all girls who had to grow up quicker than usual. Because of that, we all thought we were grown! We were all in our early teen years with old souls; we understood each other differently in that way.

Every once in a while, a few of the girls would get brave and try to run away from the house, which never worked out for them. The funniest time was when two of them ran away in their bath towels! Mind you, the facility was in the middle of nowhere within Amish country. Somehow, they hitched a ride with someone, but ended up in a public place where they were found. I'm not sure how far they thought they were going to get in their towels; I think it was less than an hour before they were brought back!

There were very scary moments, too. Another girl tried to beat the night staff with the pots and pans in the kitchen one night. The next morning, we woke up to her saying goodbye to us in handcuffs; she was transferred to Kids First, and we never saw her again. I saw more than I should have while staying there, and most of the time, it scared the living daylights out of me. On the flip side, it made me feel a lot better about myself, knowing I wasn't struggling with a lot of the mental health struggles I was surrounded by. I always felt like it could have been worse, even though I just had a different cup of crazy. None of us were better or worse than the other, we just had different cups.

Although it was undoubtedly difficult being in there, the staff structured it as best they could to make it feel like normal life. I genuinely have so many fond memories! We went rock-climbing, went to church twice a week, to the gym, and went on walks. I learned more than I ever had about cooking from different cultures, cleaning, and how to live a balanced life. Some of the girls in there with me became like sisters, and many of the staff were such special people. Those women prayed with me, encouraged me, disciplined me, loved me, and truly treated me as if I were their own daughter. The things I learned from those Jesus-loving women are invaluable!

Seven months in, I had passed all my levels, and it was finally time for me to graduate from the program and go home! After coming and going as I pleased before being in there, I felt so ready to get out after months of being told what to do and where I could be at all times. Yet, I was unprepared for what I was about to walk into at home. I had a gut feeling that there were things that still needed to be resolved between my parents. I was concerned about how that would be taken out on me. At the graduation, I was required to give a presentation in front of all the girls about passive-aggressive behavior, something that had built inside of me with my parents over many years, and that I had learned how to overcome while there. I never would have thought I was passive-aggressive with anyone, but I think I became that way with my parents after trying for so long to have my voice heard. The women at Pathway taught me to fight for my voice, which was probably one of the most important and valuable lessons I took away from my time in Pathway of Hope.

Within those seven months, I had rekindled a genuine relationship with Jesus, started to build a relationship with my dad, learned to view myself and my body the way Jesus does, discovered that my voice matters tremendously, overcame running to alcohol or drugs to cope, and felt a small level of healing in my family begin to sprout. For maybe the first time, I had unwavering hope for my future. As I prepared to speak in front of all the parents, peers, and staff present at the graduation ceremony, I felt inspired and stronger than ever. Shame was lifted and replaced with empowerment from the Lord. I was filled to the brim with joy in my spirit like nothing I could ever put into words – it was like getting a chance at life again! Even as I try to put it into words now, I can't help but be overwhelmed with tears. I can recall the joy today as palpable as it was then, even over fifteen years later. God had placed me in that program for a reason. Although those months were some of the most gut-wrenching, stretching, excruciating yet beautiful months of my life thus far, they ultimately caused me far more joy than pain.

A Slow Re-Entrance Back Into Real Life, Purity, and a Relapse

Although I was ready for new friendships after being home, I didn't know how to sever the friendships I had before going into rehab. Things also seemed to revert right back to square one between me and my parents, as well as between the two of them. A few short months after graduating from the program, at sixteen, I relapsed. Technically, I was supposed to be grounded on my sixteenth birthday, but I fabricated a story to hang out with one of my friends. My friend and I came up with what we thought was a grand plan to stuff the bed with pillows – quintessential teenager stuff right there – and snuck out the back slider doors. Did you really *live* when you were young if you didn't stuff your sheets with pillows and sneak out?! We took off our shoes, ran barefoot through all of my neighbors' lawns, and called a taxi to take us to a party a couple of miles away. I remember feeling so alive running through everyone's yards and laughing! When we got there, we were surprised that the party only consisted of two boys…but they had alcohol, which was all we were after. Oh, the wisdom of sixteen!

For as long as I can remember, it was drilled into my head that sex before marriage was a sin, to the point where I had an imaginary chastity belt throughout my teenage years. A wild party girl who could drink everyone under the table, but when it came to the three-letter word, I had sky-high boundaries. I'm thankful that mindset was seared into my brain, but no one believed me that I hadn't had sex because I was so unhinged. Literally, like a wild raccoon in a trash bag, you couldn't tell me a dang thing! Even so, it was the one thing I kept a tight lock on – thank God! I was never afraid to voice why it was something I never planned on doing until marriage, and it shocked most people. I'm so grateful I held it sacred in my heart! Which brings me back to that night at my sixteenth birthday…without too many details, it was the first time I'd really gotten too close to giving that precious gift away. With the relief of walking out of that room, sobriety smacked me in the face like a freight train. One of the guys said something about the cops coming, and I grabbed my friend, who was too drunk to walk down the stairs. After a lot of failed attempts to carry her down the stairs, I slapped her in the face as hard as I could and gave her a pep talk about how I wasn't going to rehab again. I'm laughing because it was as dramatic as it sounds, and I can't imagine how that must have sounded to her, but it worked! She marched down the stairs on her own into the taxi I had called. For as wild as I was, I had a major sense of responsibility for myself and others. Hallelujah for that; it's probably what kept me alive in many instances!

I only had a few dollars in my pocket to get us home, so the taxi driver only drove us as far as that would get us, which was to the end of my street – a pretty long walk, especially with a friend who was almost too drunk to walk herself. I didn't really think through the whole having to go back home part because, honestly, I wasn't planning on having to face that until the next day. I was very much an 'only think about the now' person. I thought I had more time to make the reprimand that I knew was coming worth my while. We ran back across all my neighbors' lawns, waking up all of their dogs in the process, while I loudly whisper-yelled at my friend to hurry up. She was hilariously drunk walk-running. When we finally got to the front door, it was locked, forcing me to ring the doorbell. It was probably around four in the morning at this point, and my dad answered the door with a wide-eyed, angry look on his face and asked me where I'd been. I made up some story about how we went for a walk in the nearby subdivision (there was a huge pond with a walkway around it) and that we were there with some friends. I think he was too tired to fight, so he didn't really challenge my excuse. He took my friend home in the morning. After that, as usual, we never spoke of it again. I waited a couple of days for one of my parents to bring it up, but it never happened.

If I could go back in time, I would high-five sixteen-year-old me for abstaining from sex over and over again and say to myself, "Yes, girl! That is precious, and you are not a gumball machine, that's a one-time gift you can't take back!" I assume it was expected that I would have put myself out there with the reputation that I had,

I'm not naive to that, but that doesn't mean I have to live up to a reputation other people have of me! I think this has created a feeling of urgency in my late twenties as I've led church groups to share with younger women the sacred spiritual connection that is sex. You are *literally* consecrating yourself to another person by consummating. Please stay with me for a second. I'm just sharing the way God intended for sex to be – good and holy!

The definition of consecrate is "to dedicate yourself to God," in simple terms.

The definition of consummate is "make (a marriage or relationship) complete by having sexual intercourse."

Another definition for consecrate is sacred. Marriage is *sacred to God*. By design, sex is a huge deal to God, therefore, it's a huge deal to us and creates a spiritual binding between us and another person. It was *created* that way! Now imagine if you've given yourself to multiple people. You have intertwined yourself, spiritually, with your very *soul*, with those people. Yes, it is *that* serious! I think teenage-me knew there was more to the picture as to why I couldn't give myself up in that way to just anyone, although I didn't fully understand just yet. Now, after working at a sex trafficking prevention organization for a short time and from what I've heard from the women in my groups, the enemy has attempted to fully derail any spiritual meaning that sex might have, in exchange for a lie. A lie, through social media, TV, music, and several other public platforms, that has tried to convince us all that it's just a quick hit, like a drive-thru. And it's cheapened sex. Satan has literally tried to convince us that sex is a one-time exchange when, in reality, you are exchanging your soul with that person. That's why we say, "until death do us part" when we get married, because, according to God, we become one flesh, we are sealed together spiritually. "For this reason a man will leave his father and mother and be united to his wife, and the two will become one flesh" (Ephesians 5:31). Our soul is powerful! God's word puts it best:

"What good will it be for someone to gain the whole world, yet forfeit their soul? Or what can anyone give in exchange for their soul?" (Matthew 16:26)

"Do not be afraid of those who kill the body but cannot kill the soul. Rather, be afraid of the One who can destroy both soul and body in hell" (Matthew 10:28).

I would encourage a deep dive into a list of scriptures of what God's word says about our souls if you're wanting to know more (I've included some in the back of this book). Our bodies are temporary, but our souls are eternal!

Childlike Joy and Stripping Away My Old Self

I was always the wild one: the one dancing to no music, running from the cops, or sleeping on the beach until the cops kicked me out. You never had to dare me twice, and I was always the first to speak my mind. Sometimes, I think fear was just nonexistent for me back then. I believe God gave me *some* of that adventurous spirit, but I know for sure that it was exaggerated or taken in the wrong direction by my flesh. I think when we're young, there are so many parts of us who are the purest, most genuine, free form of who we really are. Those parts are not meant to dissipate as we get older. As I've walked with the Lord over the course of the last several years, it took longer than it should have for me to shed the religious aspect of Jesus that *people* have taught me and instead, fully embrace childlike joy from *Jesus* that is completely free from judgment. Even Jesus tells us this! "Truly I tell you, unless you change and become like little children, you will never enter the kingdom of heaven" (Matthew 18:3).

At sixteen, one of my most memorable moments was when I quit my job on the spot because my parents were out of town for the week. I knew where the keys to the house were, as well as the keys to the car. There was fun to be had, and a job would just have to wait! I didn't have my license at the time, but that didn't stop me from driving the car around as if it were my own, or having a huge house party. Again, I thought I was all the way grown at that age! Like, dangerously. The morning after the party, I stood up on a chair and cussed everyone out for flushing balloons down the toilet, which had flooded the basement, and because someone drove their car around the lawn, leaving tire marks. I made everyone help me clean up, and I even made someone help me mow the lawn to cover up the tire marks that hilariously wavered through the backyard. I probably had a different idea of partying than my peers because flushing balloons down the toilet wasn't my idea of a cool time. Somehow, the cops didn't show up. My neighbors had to have known I was having a massive party while my parents were out of town, but maybe my driving my mom's car around threw them off. The whole thing still makes me laugh!

I distinctly remember thinking to myself, "I don't even want to have this party, but it's what people expect of me." My heart was still in the process of changing posture towards the Lord, and I wasn't brave enough yet to fully commit and put both feet in with Him. I also couldn't get it out of my head that when I decided to fully jump in with Jesus, life would be boring. No more wild parties, no more getting high with a bottle of Burnett's until five in the morning (which honestly sounds like torture to me now). It took a while to realize that letting go of those things would bring about the real peace I had been seeking all along. Along with an indescribable, childlike joy that could have only come from Jesus!

The Cindy Saga Continues

I wasn't often living at home after rehab since my mom and I could barely look at each other without an argument flaring up about absolutely nothing. She always looked at me with disdain, and I could feel that my presence wasn't wanted from a mile away. I made it a point to only be there when Dad was visiting from work in Arizona, which was about every other weekend. The rest of the time, I was in and out of the house.

Remember my Mom's BFF, Cindy? She was still very much a looming presence. She particularly didn't like that my family was happy, or at least looked to be happy. Maybe from the outside, she thought that my mom had the total package, and that may have made her jealous. Her first husband had died, her daughter had been in a car accident and burned alive as a child, and she had had to take on the role of mother to her siblings at an unusually young age. At least, that's what she told my mom, but we'll never know if that's the truth or not. I think that's why she chose my mom – a very vulnerable individual who was seeking a maternal figure. She was constantly in my mom's ear, spewing lies about my dad cheating, lying, or doing things he wasn't actually doing. She spread rumors and tore down each member of my family because she knew my naive mom would soak it up like a sponge. This woman had my mom mentally trapped, and because of that, she was able to manipulate her like a puppet to say or feel whatever she wanted. To see Cindy's manipulation up close and personal was like watching someone with a personality disorder fight for who they really are, while slowly losing the battle. I never knew which version of my mom I would get next; I have never seen manipulation like it in my entire life.

She had been pulling strings with my mom for probably four years by this point, and I started to feel that it was larger than just an unhealthy imitation of a mother-daughter relationship – it was spiritual. Not only could I see it, I could *feel* it when Cindy was around. As cheesy as it might sound, it was as if this woman had cast a spell on my mom, and she slowly became bitter, cold, and quite literally began to look like Cindy herself (I told ya it was going to be like a telenovela). She started to look *just* like Cindy. I am not kidding. I came home from school while living at home for a short stint, and, seeing a wig on the kitchen table, I asked, "Um, Mom... what is this thing?" It looked like Donald Trump had taken off his wig and deserted it right there on our kitchen table. Or maybe even like a small guinea pig had died there! She lit up with excitement and said, "Oh, that's my new wig from Cindy! It's the same color as her hair, and I got my hair colored like hers, too! Do you like it?" The best I can describe my facial expression would be a mix of sheer disgust and confusion. Within the next few months, she started to shop where Cindy shopped, bought the same things, wore the same makeup…it was like a one-sided *Freaky Friday*. She spent every day either on the phone for hours with her, or they were at each other's houses.

Dad was working and living out of state and had no idea what was really going on. Cindy took advantage of that and worked her way into my mom's heart and home, right underneath my dad's nose. My mom had transformed into a completely different person, and he wasn't even there to witness the butterfly effect afterwards.

The lessons I learned while watching the unhealthy relationship unfold between Mom and Cindy for over five years have stayed with me. Not everyone is your friend, and not everyone is *for* you. It's still kind of mind-blowing to me that there are women who could do what Cindy does for sport. God's word says that there are women like this and even warns us that they *worm their way into homes*. "They are the kind who worm their way into homes and gain control over gullible women, who are loaded down with sins and are swayed by all kinds of evil desires" (2 Timothy 3:6). I'm not speaking out of being jaded from experience, because I can assure you that I used to be. Instead, I'm speaking from a place of healing. The Bible has taught me to test every spirit (1 John 4:1), and that if we walk with the wise, we will become wise, but if we're a companion of fools, we will suffer harm (Proverbs 13:20). I saw both of those scriptures play out in real time. I'm not trying to dog on my Mom but it sure did teach me to be alert and aware of people who aren't for me. 1 Peter 5:8 tells us, "Be alert and of sober mind. Your enemy, the devil, prowls around like a roaring lion looking for someone to devour." Sometimes people come in looking like sheep, so we have to be discerning and set boundaries! I can confidently say that when things got really bad and my mom became bitter, unfortunately, she was not *for* me. That was evident. Something spiritual had happened in her heart, and although I didn't fully grasp exactly what it was, God gave me the know-how to protect myself from it at all costs.

Searching for "Home"

Home was not my *home* anytime that I was there. I was intentionally trying to be anywhere else to find a semblance of what felt like a semi-healthy version of "home." Whoever would allow me to live with them, I was there because anywhere was better than being at "home." It had already been a few years of couch surfing for months at a time, but it continued as my home life became something that I could not allow myself to be around. The following few years of my teenagehood were spent running to safety, love (or an illusion of it), and numbing myself with alcohol and drugs.

During the short stints of being home, I was constantly confined to my bedroom or grounded for anything my mom (and Cindy) could think of. If I came out of my room for any reason, they badmouthed me as if I weren't in the room. I kind of felt like Cinderella: hated, unprotected, and unsafe. I was in constant fear that the next time I walked out of my bedroom to go to the bathroom, she would flip and tell me to leave the house again. She was not mentally stable; I never knew what emotion would pop up next with her. I had to get out, I had to protect myself. With

Dad living in Arizona, the only thing I knew how to do in that situation was run.

One Saturday, I'd had enough and devised a plan to get the heck out, but didn't yet have a couch to crash on. I called a friend to come and pick me up, packed a small bag full of clothes with my mom's cell phone (I didn't have my own at the time), shoved it all out the window, and jumped out after it. I walked down the street as fast as I could and hid behind a tree, chain-smoking and eating the pizza I had grabbed from the kitchen beforehand. I'm laughing to myself now for how fearlessly I walked down the street to my hiding place in the bushes with pizza in one hand and a cigarette in the other, all while giving no conscious thought to what I was actually doing. All that was rolling through my head was a big, blaring "MUST ESCAPE" sign. *I had to protect myself.* It was the first time I had really run away from home.

My friend showed up a long thirty minutes later, and by the end of the night, I was at a different friend's house, who I would live with for the next couple of months, Anna. She had a cute, small apartment downtown, and after I explained my situation, she empathized with me and offered to let me stay as long as I needed. I didn't plan on staying away from home for a few months, but I felt that I had to do something drastic to make my Dad – or anyone – understand the gravity of what was going on at home. I didn't have a cell phone like most of my friends did at sixteen, which was why I had grabbed my mom's phone on my way out, knowing my dad would call at some point.

Dad called repeatedly two days later, but there was no snowball's chance in Hell that I was going to let him know where I was. I also wasn't going to give him any opportunity to try and talk me into going home. I ignored all of his calls for two weeks. My mom called twice, leaving two nasty voicemails about how the cops would be looking for me. When I finally calmed down enough and decided I was ready to give Dad a call back, he was angry, but he listened. As expected, he tried to convince me to go home and that we'd all sit down as a family to talk about it when he was home for a weekend. Living and working in Arizona at the time, he flew home to Michigan when he could. I told him it was too late to sit down and chat; if he'd been present for what had been going on the last several months at home, then he would understand why I had had no choice but to leave! When he started to yell, I hung up. I wasn't playing anymore. I had to take a polarizing stance for myself. You were either going to protect me, or I was going to do it myself to the best of my abilities. As a sixteen-year-old, that was a very strange place to mentally have to be. The development of self-preservation started early because of the extent to which I had to go in order to protect my overall well-being. I now know that this was why I'd started to put walls up around myself against people. What started at thirteen was only being exacerbated. I became a wrecking ball somewhere in between trying to maintain the fun-loving, teenage girl I should have been, and growing up too quickly because there was no other option. I had to advocate for myself because no one else would.

Life during those two long months living with Anna was a carefree, drunken blur with some of the best and worst memories. I lived in Anna's spare bedroom, had no money, no conscience, and a lot of anger. I was hanging out with a different guy almost every night, trying to fill the void of feeling loved and valued. Anna and I would chainsmoke in her tiny smoke room and talk into the wee hours of the morning about our dreams of what we hoped our lives would eventually look like. Every weekend, we would go out to Muskegon for parties and get obliterated. I remember bits and pieces of those parties, but not much; I was drinking more than I ever had in my entire life. I could polish off a fifth of vodka, smoke a couple blunts, and you couldn't tell the difference between that version of Tori or sober Tori. It was a confusing line that I didn't want to be on the sober side of. My personality was always over-the-top, and I have always been funny and goofy, which was probably why most of my peers always thought I was drunk or on something, even when I was sober.

We were at a house party one night with a bunch of people we had never met before, like any other weekend. I drank a fifth, some beers, and smoked too much, so I went upstairs to sleep it off. I was the only one upstairs until I felt someone on top of me. I was so drunk and high that I literally could not see straight or move a muscle in my body. My entire body was limp, and I couldn't speak. In hindsight, I'm pretty sure that I was drugged. Just in the nick of time, Anna walked up the stairs and yelled at the guy on top of me, "What the hell are you doing?" and he replied with some gross story about how I wanted to hook up with him, which, obviously, I would have never consented to. If Anna hadn't walked up the stairs when she did, I don't even want to think about what could have happened. Less than an hour later, I was back at it with a blunt in my hand, dancing around their kitchen, trying to ignore what I could remember of what had just happened.

There are so many moments that I can recall where I know without a doubt in my mind, God was blocking the worst that could have happened to me! There were too many mornings that I woke up, looked at the trainwreck of smeared mascara all over my face in the mirror, listened to the stories my friends would tell me about my antics from the night before, and I'd wonder, "How do I not remember that?"

It was August by then. Two months of partying, forgetting what day it was, and trying to fill the void of anger with alcohol started to morph into depression. Communication from my parents was few and far between, with an occasional threatening voicemail from my mom saying, "The cops are out looking for you and they will find you." All I know is, if the cops truly had been looking for me in the microscopic town of Grand Haven for months and didn't find me roaming around chain-smoking by then, they must not have been looking very hard!

Juvie and the Presence of the Lord

One of my friends from school, Christie, lived with her aunt, and by the end of the two months or so, I had overstayed my welcome at Anna's. I stuffed everything I had into my trusty cardboard box and stayed with Christie at her aunt's house for one night before deciding that it was time to face going home. Afraid of what was waiting for me behind the front door, Christie's aunt dropped me off in the driveway. I rang the doorbell and felt my body tense up, as if preparing for a fight. My mom opened the door, looked at me with narrowed eyes without saying a word, swung the door wide open, and walked away. She didn't say anything to me the rest of that day. I could hear her talking on the phone, and I knew it was Cindy on the other end, no doubt feeding my mom some crazy spoonful about what her next move should be. I made a pizza and fell asleep on the couch in the basement, exhausted from being in survival mode for so long. It was like catching up on two months of lost sleep, and strangely, the feeling of being home made me feel somewhat settled inside. I knew it was only temporary, but I sat in the dark of the basement in silence and took the moments to relish in the peace and quiet.

That good feeling didn't last long, as I woke up a couple of hours later to a police officer. I was totally blindsided, though I knew to expect the unexpected as long as Cindy was advising my mom. My mom didn't say one word to me, and I wasn't exactly sure why I was being handcuffed, except that I was considered a runaway. As far as I was concerned, I was back! In my head, I had hoped for some prodigal daughter moment, or at the very least, she would have expressed concern or excitement that I was now home. Her lack of any emotion was very telling for me.

The officer handcuffed me and walked me out to the driveway. After he put me in the backseat, he turned around to look at me and said, "Tori, I really don't want to do this because I know your mom…she's been calling us every chance she can to try and have you arrested for the past year; I'm not sure what you did to get on her bad side, but you really must have done something." I didn't say anything back to him. This dude had no idea, and I was accustomed to adults giving me the runaround, so I wasn't going to waste my breath trying to explain the situation. Would he even listen? Would he have believed me? I wasn't unaware of how crazy it would all sound, like an episode of Jerry Springer. All I knew was, I was getting locked up for a bit, and I wasn't sure what to expect. My walls kept rising, and my view of the world was skewing. I could feel my emotions bounce between rage and deep sadness. I wondered, if I stood on a table with a megaphone, would someone listen to me then?

There's no way to describe the feeling of wearing a blue jumpsuit with handcuffs on and shackles on your feet while trying to walk into a small room with a judge who holds your future in their hands. Inhumane. Humbling. I felt like an animal chained up as I sat in the chair next to my mom in a little room, awaiting the judge. As she started asking questions, my mom jumped at every chance she could to tell her how "bad of a kid" I'd been with the party I had had at the house while they were on vacation. It felt like the only thing she didn't blatantly say was, 'My daughter is the worst thing that ever happened to me, and she's the reason I'm so miserable.' I laid it all out for the judge, there wasn't anything to lie about. I was too tired to fight with my mom or to try to stand up for myself. I felt defeated, like there was no one in the world who was in my corner. Luckily, the judge said I would just need to do 7-10 days. I won't lie, it was terrifying for a girl who never went a day without a full face of makeup on, as bougie as that may sound. Although I was always moving from place to place, I knew how to take care of myself and look presentable. Most of the time, that meant getting ready in my car or a public bathroom. But juvie scared me; someone stripping my comfort of appearance from me was good in a way, because I couldn't do anything but focus on the inside, rather than putting on a physical facade that looked as if everything was fine.

My little cell was equipped to the nines with a silver toilet, a Bible, and a small cot. Truly magazine-worthy. To my surprise, it wasn't all that bad. I wouldn't vacation there by any means, but it certainly could have been worse. At least I didn't have to pee in front of strangers!

After a couple of days, I really had time to process everything that had unfolded over the last year. For the first time, I wasn't hustling to figure out where my next meal was coming from or if I had overstayed my welcome at the place I was temporarily living. I had to ponder how I got to where I was and at what point my relationship with God had fallen apart. I was so angry with Him. How could this "good God" I felt like I knew before leave me abandoned again with parents who were absent, and a mother who hated me? Where was God in any of it?

I was shocked when one of the staff came and got me for visiting hours. Thinking it might have been my parents, I was surprised to see my old youth pastor from private school walk through the door. I don't think I'd seen him for about a year or more, so it was especially weird to see him paying me a visit in juvie. He had always been kind, soft-spoken, and offered advice without judgment, which was exactly what he offered during our short visit. I cried to him and opened up my heart in a way I hadn't to any adult, because I'd grown to distrust adults. I needed someone like him who wouldn't judge, who would respect my side of the story, and genuinely listen. He gave some great insight while reminding me how much God loved me. I didn't know until that moment how much these words needed to be heard: "God loves you so much, Tori." It was almost like I had forgotten. I was so deeply encouraged by his visit, and there is no question in my mind that God had sent him. There were about seven days left in my stay, and all of a sudden, I was on fire for the word of God. The fire was lit again! Every little bit of free time we would get during the day, I would ask for the Bible from my cell. Every night was spent in my cell, crying at the feet of Jesus until the morning, clutching my Bible to sleep. His word became precious and life-giving to me in a way they hadn't before! Little did I know that was just another step in the process of my heart being pruned and softened towards God. He still had a lot more to unwind in me.

My parents came in to visit once during visiting hours – I was shocked to see them! It was a rough thirty-minute visit, but somewhat positive, nevertheless. I knew in my heart that I was not the root of the problem or their marriage, but like a neon sign in my face, I was again reminded that there was so much more going on with them. It felt like all the work that had been put in at Pathway in counseling sessions had slipped away for them, especially in regards to their relationship with me. It wasn't safe for me to be in an environment with them, especially to live at home. Blaming me, each other, and refusing to take responsibility for themselves still, I knew going back home would have been going back to the toxicity, but I also didn't have anywhere else to go then. My main goal was to get my heart and head right enough to where I could live, work, and survive on my own, separate from my parents. I knew I had trauma to heal from, and that I would need some helping hands to get a leg up in life. I clung to God and gave Him my mustard seed of faith. I hoped that He would come through, but I didn't have the best track record of trusting anyone. The beauty was, He knew that. And He knew exactly how to fix it.

Spending my seventeenth birthday in juvie was like being on an episode of *Punk'd*. The staff handed me a Watchamacallit candy bar, said "Happy Birthday," and then told me I could possibly be transferred to jail since I was now considered an adult in the system. I only had a few days left before being released, so it would have been ridiculous. Part of me was waiting for Ashton Kutcher to pop out of the corner and yell, "You've been Punk'd!" It's obviously not where I imagined I would be at seventeen!

For the next couple of days, I had anxiety until I found out that I wouldn't be transferred to jail. I was released a day later, and I didn't expect much to change at home, but the long shower I took once I got home was the most gloriously clean time of my life after having five-minute timed showers!

Out with the Old, In with the New: Another Stepping Stone to Jesus

It had been a little over a year since my seven months in rehab, and salvaging friendships that had faded out seemed like a waste of time. My experiences had put me at a different maturity level than my peers. I found it so hard to relate to most of the people my age. I was seeking mature friendships, those who had been through some real-life life, like myself. I wanted to find people who were looking for more out of life. I didn't know then, but what I was really seeking was holy friendships with a heart for the Lord. I just didn't know where to start! When you go through such intense life issues at a young age, I think it makes you cherish simple things a lot more. I wanted to find people around me with the same mindset.

I started to look for people that I would vibe with, completely aware that I had now become 'that girl that disappeared and went to rehab.' I had a self-revelation that I was the friend some of my friends' moms didn't want their kids hanging out with. As a mama now, I would say touche to those moms, I get it, I really do!

However, being so far through the thick of the mess now, it's given me clarity to know that there's always more to the story. It's taught me to throw judgment out the window, because there is *always* a more complex picture behind that painted door. And most importantly, to have grace and allow room for mistakes, especially with younger, impressionable minds. We can teach our kids morals, right and wrong, and even give them a playbook to life, but at the end of the day, they're going to be a teenager and I personally want my kids to be able to look back on their younger years and laugh at some fun, even wild, memories they made!

I was living at home for probably the longest stint of time that I ever had then, probably about a month. It made it easier to make new friends and let go of the old. It was time to cut ties with a lot of them, to finally put a line in the sand and begin a different stage of life for myself. That meant surrounding myself with new people!

I only remember bits and pieces of how it happened, but I met up with a girl that I didn't know all that well from a different local school. Lex and I grabbed a pizza, and almost instantly, we were inseparable. Remember when it was just that breezy to make friends? It was so much easier to do when we were young! I think Lex and I collided at the perfect time in both of our lives, where we were searching for growth. We were kindred spirits in many ways, struggling through some of the same things: drugs, family issues. We were like two peas in a pod, connected by our past and pain. We truly clicked, like sisters. We loved music, art, getting high, and rolling with the punches of life. What a different world, ha! It was a key friendship that taught me sisterhood, and on the flip side, how dangerous it can be when you're both self-medicating and enabling one another. We were perpetuating and suppressing pain, and I'm not sure either of us was aware of it at the time. For about four years, we were joined at the hip, with a side of some trauma bonding in there. All the experimenting with drugs and supporting each other at the same time was both comforting and a negative spiral.

As they had a history of doing, things at home hit a wall, so I ended up living with Lex and her mom sporadically for a few months. If I didn't have somewhere to go, I knew I had a bed there. Whenever I was there, I felt comfortable. Her mom was an alcoholic, so that fed into things for all of us. I don't fully remember a lot of nights, but I do remember feeling safe with my sister-friend. Her parents were separated, and when I was in a pinch again about a month later, I ended up staying a short while at her Dad's house with their family. Lex was truly my family. There was something powerful and healing in knowing that she always had my back and I always had hers. In a lot of ways, our friendship helped me to trust people again.

Lex and I were really tight with a group of about five guys, who all became like brothers to us over time. We hung out every chance we had, always driving around aimlessly, getting high, singing Blink-182 songs at the top of our lungs. I remember those moments like the back of my hand! We all became like brothers and sisters. There's something good in everything, and those little pockets with those special people still make me smile: moments like lying in the middle of an old abandoned field of wheat grass, getting high and singing to the Beatles. How funny that in those moments, I thought that that was all there was to life! Our worlds are so small when we're that young.

I became very close with one of the guys we hung out with, Derek. I knew him through mutual friends, but we didn't start to hang out until midway through high school. He and I had a different bond, but because I was seeking validation from a relationship with a guy, he had way too much power over my emotions. I never told him how I felt, and looking back, it would have been a mistake at that time in our lives. It got harder to keep it quiet, though. I started to get to know him deeper and love who he was. His family had a way of making me feel like I mattered, like there was a safe haven where I could get grounded. It seemed like no matter what rocks were thrown at me throughout that season of life, Derek could somehow put the scattered pieces back where they belonged. Cue all the big, dramatic teenage feelings!

He was such a blessing through that short, rough patch in my life. I had moved in and out of over five different places within the course of about seven months, as I was really getting to know him, and he was a steady constant. I don't think he understood why I was always couch surfing from place to place, and I didn't really want to explain more than the facts. I stayed quiet about my feelings for him for a couple of years; we were best friends first, so

I wasn't going to lay my cards out on the table! I dated a few other guys in the meantime to figure out whether or not I was ready to *really* commit.

I never wanted to commit to anything, relationship-wise. To me, everything was temporary because at that time, everything in my life was! Commitment? Didn't know her. You could not hold me down, and the second any guy I was dating tried to, I was out. A long-term relationship was like someone putting me in a glass bottle and corking the top. I had no idea what settling down meant or felt like, and had no intention of trying to find out. I was comfortable controlling who got past the iron gates of my heart, and almost no one was allowed in there! It was self-preservation, the only way I knew how to protect myself, even though I was actually self-sabotaging by never allowing anyone in. Once I did let someone in, I cut it off immediately because I was too afraid that someone would see how shattered my life was, and that I, in fact, did not have it all together like I tried to appear to.

No Roots

Couch-surfing had pretty much become a full-time job. My Mom refused to move out to Arizona with my Dad, and he was out there by himself for a really long time. She didn't want to leave her life at home, so they'd been living separately. At that time, I was barely seventeen with an older boyfriend who lived at home in Michigan. I was still in high school, but my Dad thought it would be best that I move to Arizona with him. He assumed Mom would move out there if I were there, which made me raise an eyebrow. I knew it would never happen, but I suppose he had to try. Reluctantly, I packed up a suitcase. I figured it might be nice not to have to house-hop and couch-surf. I hoped this move would be the end of that and that we'd come together as a family.

He had been staying in Arizona for over six months in an empty hotel room by himself while working. I could see that it had taken a toll on him. Just one week into living with him in Arizona, just starting to grasp the idea of settling in, Dad decided that he couldn't keep going without my Mom there. Just like that, he quit his job, and we were moving back home. What a whirlwind that week was!

My world was constantly shifting at what felt like the speed of light. I was always being jerked around in every direction, and in some ways, it was exciting to me. On the other hand, there was no steady space for me. I grew accustomed to my world being flipped upside down, and I never knew when it was going to happen. It became my normal to have a life that had no roots.

I was happy to be back home for the time being, as I was able to see my then-boyfriend. Having a relationship gave me something to focus on. Dad was right back in the computer chair, searching for a job again. It wasn't long before he had decided to take a chance and invest in a company in Texas. For me, that meant moving to and living in Houston, the same scenario as Arizona. Again, my mom refused to move with him, staying home in Michigan.

Nomad Life + A Christmas Revelation

Between the ages of fourteen and nineteen, I had moved about sixteen times, if you want to count all the couches I had stayed on, friends' houses I had lived at, the tossing between family's houses, and living in my car. It was a vacillation between living with anyone who would take me and how many days I was allowed to be at home until my Mom decided to kick me out again. It usually was never more than a week at home, and I was gone for months again. There were times when Mom wouldn't allow me home for months, but then would change her mind. Consistency was a completely foreign concept for me.

On one occasion, I was living with a friend in high school, Callie. She was equally in need of some guidance and was grappling with addiction, like I was. My brother, who lived in California at the time, had come home for Christmas while I was still living with Callie. During those tough times, my brother became one of the only people I called when I was in trouble. He didn't understand how much had happened at home or all the details of Mom and Dad's spiral. He especially didn't grasp how it was for me to be caught in the midst of everything. How could he, while living so far away? I didn't expect him to.

I called him on Christmas Day to wish him Merry Christmas; he was in town, but I wasn't allowed home at that time. He was appalled to find out that my Mom had banned me from being at home with family on Christmas Day, and he somehow convinced her that I could come home for just a couple of hours. What I hadn't told my brother was that things were at their worst for me, mentally. Everything was starting to physically wear on me, and I no longer felt like I could keep it together. The night prior, I had taken a pretty big concoction of drugs with alcohol. I was to the point where I had no regard for myself, and it genuinely seemed like no one else did either. It's a miracle I woke up the next morning, and the only explanation is that God was protecting me!

I didn't really want to go home for Christmas. It was more comfortable for me to be in any other environment than where my mom was, regardless of how bad that environment was. She had made it clear that I wouldn't be receiving any presents because I didn't deserve them. I couldn't grasp why my own mother had so much hatred towards me.

When my brother picked me up, I was still strung out from the night before, which made seeing my family that much more difficult. Watching them open presents, laughing, and enjoying each other's company while I just sat in the corner and watched is something that will always be seared into my memory.

Everything comes back to a movie reference for me–you know the first *Harry Potter* movie, where Harry is required to make breakfast for the family he's living with while they all laugh and celebrate? It's kind of a funny parallel, but that's how it felt, like I was the unwanted daughter. Only for the sake of appearances and to make it seem like they were trying with me, I was allowed the afternoon to be home for the holiday. I will never understand the lack of love from my parents, or what I did to create the animosity towards me to such a dramatic extent. I also didn't recognize that while I had been away on and off for a few years, my family was changing too. I wasn't the only one who saw the trickle effect that Cindy was having on my Mom. It was starting to pull the seams apart in our family. On one hand, that made me grateful – I thought maybe now someone would see that everything wasn't my fault. On the other hand, it was aggravating. I wanted to fight for my family, but I couldn't! My brother brought me back to Callie's house after a couple of hours of awkwardly sitting on the floor watching them converse. I don't think any of us realized that that would be the last time my family would all be together in the same room for the next five years.

I was always high, drunk, or experimenting with drugs to find the magic cure that would deliver me from the hand I was dealt. I remember one time being on acid, while drunk and also on pills – Callie had taken a picture of us and showed it to me the next day. I was horrified at what I saw. My face was sunken in slightly and my eyes were barely open, I looked half alive! *Is that really me?* I thought. Disappointed, I laughed it off and just thought, *well, what else am I supposed to do to survive?* I didn't know how to live life without being high on something, and although it made me sad for myself. I didn't know how to stop.

After living with Callie for about a month, we were at a party that was raided by the cops after thirty minutes of being there, and we all had to blow for breathalyzers. I had only had one beer, but Callie was way past me; she blew enough to be taken to juvie since she was still sixteen. By the grace of God, I got off with no charge.

It was around one in the morning, and the cop said I could call someone to pick me up. I called a close guy friend, Rob, and ended up staying with him for a few days while the dust settled. I had no idea how long I'd be there and no plan. My little box of clothes was at Callie's house, and I wasn't sure if I would still be welcome there without her. None of us knew how long she would be in juvie, but her Mom said it would be at least a couple of weeks. I had Rob drop me off, hoping for the best, and Callie's Mom kindly welcomed me in. She graciously allowed me to stay at their home while we waited for Callie to come home. She was so kind to me, even though she didn't understand my situation. She didn't ask many questions either, which was somewhat odd to me, but I was thankful not to have to explain. She dropped me off and picked me up from school for the next two weeks without much of a conversation about it. When Callie got out and came home two weeks later, I ended up staying a little longer. All in, I was probably there for at least two or three months.

At my wits' end and tired of drowning in drugs, I reached out to my Dad. Since I was nearing high school graduation, it was dawning on me that there were no college plans on my horizon, and I wasn't too sure about the state of my family either. I wanted more, I just didn't know how to get there without any support or help. After a few conversations over the phone, Dad convinced my Mom to let me move back home once again.

My Buddy the Box, It Gets Worse Before It Gets Better

There was this large brown cardboard moving box I kept in my closet that I never fully unpacked when I moved or stayed somewhere. A lot of times, I wouldn't even move it from the trunk of my car into the place I was staying because I knew it wouldn't be long until the next spot. I would always pack as much into it as possible and live off of whatever clothes were inside until the next time I returned home to swap them out. It might be strange, but every time I looked at that brown box, I thought to myself, "Well, at least that's consistent!" I can laugh about it now; of course, it was a sad thing, but it was truly the only thing that seemed to stick with me. I even kept it a couple of years into being married because I had an attachment to that silly, torn-up box.

I also had a slight fear that marriage was temporary too, and that I may need that box again – which of course was not true. After almost ten years of marriage and a lot of incredible therapy, I've discovered that unresolved abandonment issues can make you do some weird stuff. That box represented the one thing that stayed with me through my teens for *years afterwards*. I still remember the liberating moment I decided to break that tattered box down and toss it into the trash. I was surprised that I cried! It was, strangely, very emotional for me. Who knew a cardboard box could hold so much – literally *and* figuratively. Man, am I grateful for God's restoration and healing of my broken, abandoned heart.

It was a few months before the arguing between my Mom and me became intolerable while living back home. I was being accused almost every day of doing something that I never did, as per usual, and I was burned out with frustration. She was angrier than I'd ever seen her, and something didn't feel right being around her. Even though at that time I was wishy-washy with the Lord, I felt something spiritually off around her, and it was palpable.

One night, I walked down to the laundry room at the other end of the house while she was doing laundry, and it looked like she had been crying. I walked past her and grabbed the clothes I needed. Out of nowhere, she began aggressively accusing me and verbally attacking me. But none of it made sense! It was bizarre and terrifying. She followed me out of the laundry room and body-slammed me from behind.

I turned around and said, "What are you trying to do?! You're making no sense! What is going on?"

She got about an inch from my face and yelled, "Hit me, Tori! I know you want to, hit me!"

I knew she was trying to provoke me. I knew Cindy had put the idea in her head to get her to try and have me hit her (which I would never do under any circumstances) so that she could call the cops and have me arrested. It was always about having me arrested and put in jail because she thought I "needed a lesson." After she tried to force me to hit her, I *ran* to my bedroom, locked the door, and put my vanity chair underneath it. Mortified, I thought about calling the cops. But without a phone in the room and knowing she would lie to the cops anyway, I stayed next to the door to try and hold the lock down. I knew that I'd have to defend myself if necessary, but my best option was to get out, for fear of what lie she would tell to the cops if something did happen.

My mom had never been physically aggressive or abusive before, so when she busted through the door, pushing from one side of the door while I pushed from the opposite side to keep her out, there were a million thoughts going through my head. What was happening? I knew this wasn't who she *really* was. How could I get her to snap out of this? My heart was racing, and I went into fight-or-flight mode, looking for ways to jump out the window, trying to consider where I would go once I had. I pushed back hard enough to quickly push the lock down on the doorknob. There was silence on the other side of the door. I sat in my vanity chair for a second, looking at myself in the mirror, trying to scramble together an idea of what to do next. Before another thought, my mom busted through the door, walked up to me, and pushed my chair back without saying a word. My bed was directly behind me, and I knew if I fell back, I would hit my head on the bed frame. To prevent the possibility of cracking my head open, I grabbed her shirt to pull myself back up. After pulling myself up enough and steadying the chair, I genuinely thought she might try to kill me. Instead, she paused, laughed, then looked me in the eyes and said, "I gotcha now!" Totally puzzled and petrified, I asked, "What are you talking about?!" She didn't say anything else and slammed my door shut on her way out. I immediately ran out of my room to get the landline phone as fast as I could, locked myself in my bedroom with the chair underneath the doorknob again, and tried calling my Dad. I was not surprised to hear my mom already on the phone when I clicked the phone on. She was crying while fabricating some insane story about how I had hit her. The thought of ending things for myself crossed my mind; I wondered if it would be easier. I saw no light at the end of the tunnel to this vicious cycle of survival and abuse.

I felt defeated. Powerless, unbelievably unloved, but most of all, I felt trapped – physically and mentally trapped. I tried explaining to my dad while she kept lying through her teeth on the phone. We just kept yelling over each other as my Dad kept shouting, "Stop, stop!" I felt flight mode turn into fight, I wasn't going to give up and allow her to continue lying. Unable to get a word in, my Dad finally hung up. He called back, and my Mom answered and told him her outlandish story about what had just happened as I listened from the other room. I sobbed for hours into my pillow with the chair still under the locked door. I was terrified that it wasn't over yet. This was when I knew, without a shadow of a doubt, something spiritual in her heart had changed. In retrospect, I now know it had been for quite some time, but I had just recognized it then. I remember praying, "God, my mom just tried to kill me! What else is there? What else can happen to me? I have nothing left. I have no one who believes me. Help me!" I told Him that a real God would never have allowed this to happen to me. If He was supposed to protect me, it certainly wasn't happening, and if He loved me, I for freaking sure didn't see it. Sadly, I'd told Him that I was done and renounced Him. This was my breaking point. I'd hit a wall and forfeited God altogether. It still leaves a pit in my stomach to think about.

God was with me all along, but even now, it's hard to see where He was when I felt like I had been abandoned in a pit without a ladder. There was still redemption to be had though! God was not done, even if I was! He chased after me, because He was, and is, my ultimate father!

It was around two in the morning when I woke up after painting my pillow with mascara tears in my sleep. I called Lex to tell her everything that happened, and she asked if she could come and pick me up. I was so scared to leave my room. At that point, I wasn't sure what to expect from my mom or what she was capable of. Lex and I stayed on the phone until we both fell asleep. I couldn't stay there, I knew I wasn't safe, so I packed up my cardboard box the next day. I asked Lex to pick me up when my mom wasn't home, and I went to stay with her family again.

A few days into living with them, I overheard a heated conversation coming from the kitchen about how my name was in the paper for a court appearance. I was supposed to show up in court for another Minor in Possession charge for alcohol. A friend and I got busted drinking in a public parking lot a month earlier. I was honest with her Mom, and she agreed to let me stay for one more week. This was the start of a never-ending ping-pong of being at home and then somewhere else for a week or two at a time, and back home. I had been used to a couple of months between places, so only having one week here or there was even more exhausting. I really longed for stability. My poor cardboard box was getting quite the workout!

I got used to making the public bathrooms downtown my place to get ready every morning. I'd leave wherever I was living – or my car – to do my makeup and grab clothes out of the box from the backseat of my car. At least there were really great mirrors in those bathrooms! If I were in limbo, that was my spot. They were usually empty and heated. I knew I could get warm there if it was too late, and I had nowhere to stay except for my car when it was cold.

It was winter and *ridiculously* cold one night, and I'll never forget how bone-chillingly cold it was. I had been out with a friend at the club, and I wasn't able to crash at her house for the night afterwards. I was in limbo, trying to figure out where I was going to live temporarily next, so I was sleeping in my car. I had slept in my car on cold nights before, but not during a freeze! It was so cold that my car's heat seemed like it could barely keep up. I had just a few dollars in my bag and a dang near-empty gas tank. After trying to sleep and stay warm for hours in a parking lot, the only option I had was to call Dad. There was no way for me to keep the car on and keep from freezing or running out of gas.

It must have been around three or four in the morning, but Dad answered the phone. After I explained, I could hear him roll over to ask my Mom if it was okay if I came to the house to get warm. He answered, "Just until morning, that's it". I barely made it home with my tank teetering under E. I slept until seven and was abruptly woken up and asked to leave. This is hard for me to share. Even now, I struggle to understand my parents' decisions when I had explained that I was nearly freezing, with no money or food. As a parent myself, I'll never be able to fully wrap my head around this. The amount of repeated blows of abandonment all boiled up to that moment. There was a lot of confusion with having a parent consistently be there for you until you hit teenagehood, then all of a sudden, you're their enemy. Over and over, I blamed Cindy for her influence on my Mom. What stung, though, was knowing Mom made her *own* decision to listen to that influence and consciously chose to believe the lies. She was a willing party to destroying her own family. That will always baffle me.

Making Emancipation Official

I stayed with my Grandma for a week or two after staying for a week at Lex's family's house. I'm sure she called my Dad and told him to figure it out with my Mom; she fought for me when she could. Whatever she must have said that time got me back home again.

While living at home for a hot minute, Dad was also visiting from Texas. My Mom had given him an ultimatum of signing papers to have me emancipated or sign divorce papers. She created a divisive "It's her or me" demand. Honestly, I didn't get why she even wanted emancipation papers, I barely lived there anyway. I now know it was to prevent me from living at home at all; I don't think my parents were on the same page about me not living at home. I think Dad preferred me to live at home, but gave up the fight pretty easily.

My Dad separated us because my Mom and I could not stop arguing long enough for them to have a conversation. I felt strongly, and so did she. Dad came into the guest room where I was and said, "I'm sorry, Tori, but I have to choose your Mom."

Anger welled up first inside of me, followed by sadness and fear. My heart sank as I felt another blast of abandonment. I thought for sure that my Dad would fight for me in this particular situation, and it broke my heart all over again. In hindsight, it should not have surprised me at all. I still clung to hope with everything I had that he would fight to protect me.

I sat in disbelief and stared at myself in the dresser mirror for a minute after he left the room. I can't really put into words the emotions that I felt in that moment. Deep, deep rejection and abandonment repeatedly had left me feeling numb and unable to process my feelings. I allowed myself to sit in my emotions for a moment, then forced myself to toughen up to keep moving forward. I looked at myself in the mirror and whispered, "You will not let her win, you can take care of yourself like you've been doing for a long time!" I didn't walk out of that room the same. I could no longer continue to hope that my Dad would somehow take the blinders off and protect me. There was no one I could rely on, no one who would truly listen to me or try to understand that I was being abused, both verbally and mentally. There was a good kid inside of me, stuck in a monumentally awful situation. Who would listen?! The only one who could was God. He was the only one I needed, but in my anger, I shunned Him. At the time, I felt that I had my own back, but absolutely no one else did. It was me plus me, and that's it.

I was only a little surprised when a cop was at the door thirty minutes later. He said, "I'm sorry, I have no choice but to have you leave this house. Is there anywhere I can take you?" You could tell from the look on his face that he was uncomfortable and didn't quite understand the situation himself. I begged my dad to try and have him talk some sense into my mom, but he said, "It's probably best that you leave the house, we'll figure the rest out later."

Wild + Free, Homeless Summer

Where was I supposed to go? I racked my brain. As the officer waited at the door, I went into my closet and once again packed up my well-loved, worn-out cardboard box and pushed it to the door, like many times before. Once I got to the cop car in the driveway, the officer said, "I'm here a lot more than I'd like to be." I didn't say anything. I wanted to say, "Oh, how interesting, Officer. How do you think I feel, bro!?"

As I slipped into the back of the car, next to my brown box with the belongings I'd have for the next several months, he asked, "Where to?" I didn't know until that moment. Before I could really think about whether or not it was a good idea, I told him to drop me off at my friend Courtney's house. I had met Courtney in high school, and we had become really close. Her house was the only place I knew I could stay for at least a couple of days while I figured out where to go next. Her Dad had been really kind when I'd hung out many times before, so I knew he'd let me stay for a little while. The officer dropped me off and put my box on the side of the road. I pushed it to the front door and tried simply walking in like I usually did at her house, but it was locked. She usually slept past noon, so I threw some rocks at her window to wake her up. We sat, and I told her everything. Her Dad was more than understanding and welcomed me to stay as long as I needed. I don't think any of us thought at the time that it would be a month and a half before I found another place to live!

Courtney and I were always looking for anything we could get our hands on to numb what we were going through. Kindred spirits, knee-deep in trauma, but unaware of it. She had her own set of issues that she bottled up and shoved down so far that you had to push and pull to get anything out of her. When I was younger, and even now, I was drawn to quiet people. There was something about getting to know them that made them more interesting. I've always sought out the black sheep because I was one too. To me, the black sheep and weirdos are the most fun to be around, authentic, and interesting.

The first day I met Courtney in school, she was sitting alone at lunch while I was a social butterfly, talking with anyone who would listen. She was nose-deep in a book, and I plopped down in front of her like an overly excited lab and yelled, "HEY!" I'm one thousand percent sure she was annoyed and unsure why I had interrupted her lunch hour. We were total opposites, but it worked well, and we quickly became close friends. We bonded over the painful things we were dealing with and went on weird adventures together. Living with her and her Dad honestly felt like home, which I'm so grateful to have had in the midst of my chaotic world!

We often stayed up until five in the morning, listening to music and exchanging our favorite songs. I talked and she listened while painting on her bedroom floor until we faded and slept until the next afternoon. Life was breezy and messy in the same breath. She was, and always will be, so dear to my heart.

It was clear to me that after a month and a half of being together almost all day, every day, Courtney was ready for me to leave and have her space back. I still didn't have my own cell phone, so I had been using hers. A text came through her phone as I was using it one morning – it was from her boyfriend at the time, who was bashing me. I've never been one to hold in my feelings, so I marched into her room and confronted her. Within forty-five minutes, I had called a different close friend from high school who I hadn't spoken to in a while – Emma. After explaining my situation and how I had overstayed my welcome, she said, without hesitation, "Come live with me, it will be fun!" Just like that, I packed up my beloved cardboard box of belongings again and jumped into Emma's car, onto my next journey.

Emma had a little house, just her and her little boy, in the middle of nowhere next to a blueberry field. She had recently cut off her engagement and was also trying to figure out what came next for her. For the next two months, my head was in the clouds. At first, it was a breath of fresh air being out of the center of town. I was often drinking a fifth on the hood of the car, looking at the stars until morning. The friendship, the laughter, and the rush of having no idea what each day would hold was exciting. After all, part of the excitement of life is knowing anything could happen! By then, I'd gotten comfortable and a little lazy while moving from place to place. I'd even started unpacking my box a little bit with each move. I was having the time of my life, although I was going nowhere with my future, and also dealing with the consequences from prior decisions that were really difficult to face. It was a catch-22 because I couldn't move forward and heal without dealing with my past, but it was too painful to face. It wasn't the right space or circumstance to begin healing, and I didn't know how to process pain. I only knew how to run from it.

I didn't have a driver's license at the time –the court had temporarily suspended it after I'd been caught sitting in a car with a friend, drinking on public property a few months prior. I was also required to attend AA classes at the courthouse for two months, which had conveniently started about a month after living with Emma. I thank God for how understanding Emma was of my situation, and she lent me her car whenever I needed it. She was the main reason I was able to stay out of jail by generously giving me the ability to get to those court classes!

God provided and carried me through those moments when I had no idea how I'd make it. Even though I'd abandoned Him at that time, He stayed faithful and made a way for me. It was Psalm 72:12 in real time – "For he will deliver the needy who cry out, *the afflicted who have no one to help.*"

I didn't have a choice but to drive on a suspended license. It was contradictory because I was drinking almost every day, yet going to alcohol classes that were taught by a local bartender. It made no sense! It makes me laugh now because I'm not sure how the court thought that was supposed to play out.

I lived for the in-between. The little glimmering moments of no hardship, where all of my troubles temporarily lifted. Life had no boundaries then. In so many ways, I know God was protecting me from being home at that time. I was able to live big and have fun like I should have been able to at that age, without being stifled by the dark cloud that was at home. Home was always relative. Home became *people* rather than a *place* for me, so I held them very close to my heart.

There were often times when there was no food in Emma's house, so I would run through the blueberry fields next to the house and eat as much as I could to fill my stomach. Some people might think, *How sad, she didn't even have any food to eat.* But I felt alive, free, and somehow it was all alright with me. My other friends knew I had no means of communication, being without a cell phone, so they would just show up. They would usually find me sitting in the breezeway, blowing through cigarettes or smoking a bowl to pass the time. My friends came and went as they pleased, but I was almost never alone. They'd pick me up at midnight to go off to the beach, and we'd run through the sand and skinny-dip as fast as we could before the cops came! We blasted our music in the car, singing at the top of our lungs with the windows down. *I felt so alive!*

I was reckless, but for the first time in a long, long time, I felt like I was really living rather than just being stuck in survival mode. Even though they were some of the toughest times of my life, the flashbacks of drinking too much and laughing until there were tears in my eyes with a true circle of friends around me are some of the most treasured moments of my teenage years. I'm grateful for those experiences, but I don't look back and miss them in a way of wishing I had them back. Ecclesiastes 7:10 says, "Do not say, 'Why were the old days better than these?' For it is not from wisdom that you ask about this." Being that young and outrageous will always be remembered fondly for me, but I'll never ask why "the old days were better than these." Those days and these days are just different, but nothing can compare to the love and security of walking with Jesus like I do now!

A Loving Intervention + Summer's Dramatic Close

I had a couple of caring friends who tried to rein me in and have a heart-to-heart about how out of control I was during that time. Two friends specifically woke me up a little bit to the fact that I had an alcohol problem. It's hard to take candid advice from your teenage friends who are also high and drunk while confronting you on how you have a problem. Nevertheless, it worked coming from these two specific people who I trusted.

A really close friend who had been like a brother to me sat with me on the hood of the car one night, it must have been around two in the morning. I had been drinking alone, watching the stars. He gently said, "Tori...I love you, you're important to me, and I care about you. But where do you see yourself in the future?" I laughed and asked what he meant. "You have an alcohol problem," he said as he pushed a pad of paper and a pencil towards me. I laughed and brushed it off, but didn't say anything because I knew he was right. I thought if I just kept everything suppressed, I could avoid all of my trauma and feelings. He asked me to write down my hopes and dreams for the next five years. That was honestly depressing! I remember going to bed feeling pretty low, wondering how I would ever accomplish the dreams in my heart when I just felt like a nomad, trying to figure out what my next move was. I began to believe that a life running from everything was just the way it was going to be for me. But it was so meaningful that he confronted me like he did because it sparked something in me again that reminded me that running wasn't all there was. There was a big future I was trying to hide from because I'd believed the lie that my life wasn't worth fighting for a future.

On a different morning, I was with another very close friend after I had been up all night after taking Ecstasy. She stayed up talking with me all night! She looked me in the eyes and said, "Girl, I'm worried about you, what are you doing with your life?!" That was a hard conversation. I pushed back, and so did she. She and I had been friends for five-plus years by then, so I knew she was speaking from a place of love. Two people I held close had called me out on how I was basically running from my life. Although they could never fully understand the gravity of my situation because it looked nothing like theirs, I knew they were right. Aren't you grateful for people who call you to a higher purpose? Hard conversations are worth it. God used both of those friends of mine to shake me awake!

The cookie crumbled after a little over two months of living with Emma. There was a huge festival that took place every summer where I grew up, and my friends and I were on our way to. Before we even got there, I had downed half of a fifth of vodka in twenty minutes because I thought I could tolerate it (and I thought it would be fun). I filled up my plastic cup with more as we walked around downtown. It didn't take long before the ground was spinning and I had to sit down, which had only ever happened to me once before. I could always handle my alcohol, no matter what the amount, so it took me off guard. I was with two friends at the time, who wisely knew they should bring me back to Emma's place. That was the worst alcohol poisoning I've ever had in my entire life. When I woke up the next morning, I still felt like my insides were flipped outside of my body. I genuinely thought I might die from how much I had consumed. It was probably an amalgamation of how much I'd been drinking for the past couple of months.

Emma's house had no landline, I had no cell phone, and Emma wasn't home for me to use hers. Being out in the middle of nowhere, I had no other option but to go door-to-door to see if I could use someone's phone to call home. It was humbling! I was hoping Dad would pick up since he was visiting from Houston, but my Mom answered. Of course, I wasn't going to tell her that I had alcohol poisoning and needed help. I knew she would probably try to put me in jail, given her track record. I didn't trust her, but I needed help! I told her I'd like to "talk" and asked if she would come and pick me up. She probably didn't know where I'd been for the last four or five months by that point. By a miracle of God, she agreed to pick me up thirty minutes later. We sat down to talk, and the conversation was short and went something like, "I'm sorry, and I'm ready to come home because I can't do this anymore." If I would have been honest, the conversation would have started with, "I'm sick, stuck at this house without a life, car, food, or money, and I'm tired of being drunk 24/7."

I knew I had to be careful and basically beg in order to be accepted back into the house, and that it was a long shot after Mom had had me emancipated. We came to an agreement to give it a shot again; I'm pretty positive my Dad was the one who actually fought for me to stay. I was shocked that I was allowed in after all her efforts to prevent me from being home under any circumstances. However, he got her to agree, I felt both thankful and sick because I didn't have high hopes for being allowed there for long. My busted cardboard box with a few more rips in it went back into the closet – for a little while anyway.

A Strange Scheme

Being at home at that time was eye-opening to everything that had transpired while I'd been gone for the past six months. Dad was still living out of state in Houston, so I kind of felt like a sitting duck because it felt like Cindy and my Mom had basically formed a gang. Funny, but also not funny. I was so confused that my Mom had agreed to allow me back in the house. Every time I came out of my room, the two of them were whispering about me, talking loudly about politics, or gossiping like they had before. My Mom never liked politics until Cindy, then all of a sudden, she was a critic for CNN. Cindy hated me just as much as my own mother did. I felt it every time I was home, so I made sure I was never home when they were there. The side comments from Cindy, along with the nasty things my mom would say to me, were like two catty high school girls ganging up on me. That's literally what was happening, just with adult women. It was the strangest thing to have my own mom mock, bully, and conspire against me for no good reason. Again, this is how I knew it was spiritual. It was deeply cruel and never made sense. The enemy likes to dwell in confusion and anger.

I needed to grab money out of the stash I kept in my vanity one night. My plan was to quickly run into the house and run back out without seeing either of them. I pulled into the driveway, ran in, and they were staring at me from the kitchen table. As I ran by them, I yelled that I was grabbing a sweater. After I grabbed the money, I ran through the house to get out of there as quickly as possible – it was maybe five minutes. My mom gave me the weirdest half-smile as I told her I'd be back later. I knew something was going on, but my mind couldn't handle any more games, so I chose to ignore it. I made the massive mistake of leaving a decent amount of weed in the center console of my car while I ran into the house. After I got into my car, I checked the console to see that it was gone. I knew she had taken it, which immediately explained the strange smile she gave me as I left. But I thought it was strange that she didn't say anything at all or go to war with me for finding it. I definitely wasn't going to go walk back in there (into the fire!) and ask if she had taken it – that was probably what she wanted me to do. I brushed it off and sped off to get back to my friends and smoke another joint to forget the mess I knew I'd have to deal with later.

Walking in the door later that night, I was shocked to see my mom calmly tidying up in the kitchen. There was no scolding or questioning of any kind. She just glared at me. I went back to my room and laughed to myself, thinking, "What the heck, is she keeping it to smoke for herself?" For a split second, I considered that she might be so stressed out with her life spinning out of control that she would roll one up for herself...even though all of the stress was a result of her own choices. I also wondered if she might have thrown it away. The next morning, she still hadn't said anything, and after a few days, I just forgot about it and thought we were doing that whole "If we don't talk about it, it didn't happen" thing. Turns out, she was saving it for a special occasion.

About a month later, I was at Derek's house, and someone had called his phone, asking for me. On the other end was an officer, asking me if I had had weed in my possession about a month ago. At first, I didn't know what the heck he was talking about, and then he said, "Are you sure? Because I have it right here." I lost my breath for a second, not because I was scared, but because I had so many emotions going through my head. Instantly, my mind remembered the creepy smile my mom gave me that night as I was walking out the door. Then I knew exactly what was happening: she had plotted this entire thing with Cindy the month before and waited until now. I couldn't rationalize a reason for it, though. Why? Why would she wait until a month later? I answered the officer, "Yep, it's mine." If I had that moment to do over, I would obviously deny the accusations over and over again – not out of dishonesty, but out of protection. I think I was too tired of the never-ending battle. I gave up and didn't even bother conjuring up some excuse, even though I knew without a shadow of a doubt that my own mother was setting me up. I knew I'd get a court date in the mail and that my rap sheet was messy, so jail time would be a possibility. My mom had clearly hoped for that, which made me sick, unable to fathom why she was constantly trying to get me in trouble. I was so exhausted by trying to prove to anyone that Cindy and my own mother were genuinely trying to hurt me on purpose. I was in shock for a few days that she had devised a plan to intentionally put me in jail. How do you process something so strange? I always seemed to be their target, but no matter how long I pondered it, there was no logical explanation as to why.

It came time for the court date, and I was nervous. This time though, my sweet grandma was with me. At some point after the court date was set, my mom had called my dad to share her twisted plan to get me in jail to "teach me a lesson." He wasn't having it and told my grandma so she could come with me to court since he couldn't fly back from Houston. I'm grateful she was there because that particular judge had been known for being somewhat merciless. Everyone else had been judged, and now it was just me, my grandma, and the judge in the room. Going last was absolutely a God thing. As he asked me why I was there, I wanted to scream, cry, and run – all at the same time. How could I communicate that my own parent was out to get me, with all of my examples in one summed-up answer? I didn't know how, and there wasn't enough time. At the end of the day, I was a girl who felt like she had no voice because no one had ever allowed me to have one. I felt defeated. It makes me angry that I ever allowed my mom to make me feel that way. I lowered my head and told him that the weed from the car was mine. He got quiet, then repeated, "I really should put you in jail" a few times under his breath while he rubbed his forehead, contemplating. My grandma piped up from the back of the room, begging him to try and understand that my mom had done this intentionally. After she pleaded with him a little more, he said, "Okay...I'm going to fine you, and if you can't pay that today, you'll do ninety days in jail. On top of that, you'll have six more months of probation, and I'm temporarily suspending your license again. You're lucky your grandmother is here to fight for you, or I would put you in jail." I could have sobbed, both from relief and from disappointment. I now had to call my dad to figure out how to pay for the fine or go to jail. I also felt somewhat vindicated because my mom had ensnared herself by revealing her true colors to my dad. I had hope that this was the beginning of light being shed on her intentions to hurt me. It was now undeniable: someone would have to believe me!

I called Dad from the courthouse because I had to pay in order to leave the building. I told him my options, and he kept repeating that he couldn't believe Mom would do this, she had just cost him six hundred dollars for no good reason. I knew she wouldn't be happy to hear that I wouldn't be going to jail! It finally felt like a win. I was thankful that my grandma had spoken up on my behalf! She lived out "Speak up for those who cannot speak for themselves" (Proverbs 31:8).

Texas + A Double Life

I must have only seen Dad a couple of times a month once he moved to Houston. He was basically living in two places, trying to hold it all together. It wasn't even a month after moving back home from Emma's when things took a turn with Mom, like clockwork. I found myself bouncing between places again, living between my Aunt's, my Grandma's, and our house when Dad was home, all while working a pizza job. It was so strange to only be home when my Dad was, and we weren't talking about how to make things work going forward, or if I'd ever truly be allowed to live at home again. It was just this awkward state of everything being temporary. Like, I was only allowed visiting hours at home when he was there. Dad was evidently at a loss as to how to make it work between me and Mom – which to be fair, it never could've worked at that time because she was not safe for me to be around, nor was she in a good place mentally. He recognized that Cindy was bad news, but he was also trying to keep the peace in our family, which wasn't happening, especially when Cindy was calling the shots while he was living in another state.

There were a few nights that year when I was too late for curfew for wherever I was living at that time, so I had to sleep in my car again for a bit. After enough sleepless, cold winter nights and feeling like nothing was progressing, I had reached a crossroads, and my dad decided that Houston would be my best bet. While packing up a small suitcase, I couldn't help but wonder if it would be just like Arizona, if he would quit his job again after my mom didn't follow us there. With that in mind, I packed light!

Texas really seemed like a big breath of fresh air with sunshine and a chance for me to start anew. I was excited and truly felt like it was an opportunity for a fresh start! It was a welcome change and good for my soul to get out of the toxic cycle of being tossed from place to place back home. I started off strong, had a few interviews, and even joined a cake decorating class! But like any teenager, I missed my friends. Half of my life was still in Michigan! I talked to Derek and my closest friends every night on the phone while I sat on top of the washer in the closet until morning. Somehow, Derek and I grew closer over the course of those two or so months that I lived away. I'd fly back to Michigan with my dad to see him and catch up with friends almost every weekend. Those brief visits were cherished and ended with a reality check that, like Dad, I too was living a double life in two places.

I would spend a day with Derek, then finish off the night partying with other friends, only to wake up early to catch a flight back to Houston, where my other life was supposed to be. I was trying to keep my social life intact in one place while I wasn't sure what would happen next in the other place – or if we'd even be living there for long. I knew Dad was partially using me as "incentive" again, just like he did with Arizona to get Mom to move there. I was tossed around like a salad! Part of me liked it because it was adventurous, while the other part of me continued to long for stability. I couldn't fathom the thought of calling somewhere home for long; staying in one place for too much time made me antsy, and it felt unnatural. It became habitual and started to feel like that was just the way life was.

Sin Will Take You Further Than You Ever Thought You Could Go

During one of those quick weekend trips back home to Michigan, I remember feeling like I had no control over my own life. A close friend was a drug dealer, which became an all-access pass to any drug I could think of. I was set on "opening my mind" because I thought I would find the deep answers in my subconscious that I was missing and escape the issues of life. It makes me sound like I wore Baja ponchos and said "right on" a lot. It breaks my heart that I chased so hard after all the drugs I possibly could to try and meet the thirst in my soul that could only be satisfied by Jesus. Nothing else satisfies except for Him! Especially in the dark valleys. I sure could have used Jesus in the trenches that I was in back then!

The enemy presents enticing options that look like opportunities, but they actually lead to entrapment…and it's always at the worst times. He knows how to present it with a bow and pretty wrapping, except what's inside the box hurts us. I was only worsening my pain, trying to drown it all out with any drug I could get my hands on. I know that the enemy had tricked me into thinking that the next drug would be the answer, and when that one wasn't, I believed the lie that it was just the "wrong one," when in reality, it was distraction after distraction. With each new drug came a torrential downpour of depression and shock that I couldn't numb out enough to forget my problems. My mind had not been opened, and I still didn't have the answers I'd been looking for. In fact, I felt worse with every attempt to magically *poof* all the negativity away. No matter how much I took of something or how many mixed concoctions of drugs, it wasn't fixing anything. Instead, it was driving me deeper into a pit. All I needed was to commit to Jesus to receive healing and true love! I just kept getting distracted, taking the bait from the enemy over and over.

I was still tight with Courtney, so I would see her quite a bit on the weekends that I was visiting from Houston. I was at Derek's house late one particular Saturday night, but he and my other friend didn't get along, so he dropped me off at his house. When I walked in, everyone else had already taken mushrooms, and I was determined to catch up and get the "experience" to see if you know…it would "open up my mind." Listen, if you can't laugh about your past, you'll cry. You can do both, but I'd rather laugh!

Courtney had severe anxiety, and psychedelic drugs don't mix well with anxiety! She had already been on them for a couple of hours by the time I arrived and was hiding under a blanket in the middle of a panic attack, asking if someone would take her to the emergency room. Naturally who I was back then, I quickly took what she took in hopes of catching up to her level to try and calm her down. You can't ever say I'm not a good friend, ok? I locked us both in a room to try and get through whatever was happening, because I had no idea what I was about to feel either. The room had posters plastered all over the wall of famous artists who were only freaking her out more since she started hallucinating that they were moving. I had taken mushrooms one time prior to this and had a bad trip, but knew every time was different, so I wasn't sure what to expect.

Courtney and I ended up chatting for six hours about everything you could imagine. At around four in the morning, it started to wear off; our friend came back in and offered us some white powder in a baggie, which I assumed was cocaine. He said it was a "throw-in" and he didn't know exactly what it was. Either way, I didn't pass it up, and it wasn't long before my thoughts were racing. Both Courtney and I were starting to feel strange after stacking drugs and decided to call a taxi at around five in the morning to get back to her house. I barely had enough money for the taxi ride home and was so strung out that I apparently forgot what money was when it came time to pay him! I recall forgetting what the dollars in my hand were, just sitting in the backseat of the taxi, looking at them like they were little aliens. I felt like a robot trying to remember how to count, so I gave him everything in my wallet! I still have no earthly idea how much I gave the dude, but it must have been enough! I had to catch a flight back to Texas the next morning, just a few hours from the time my head hit the pillow. As I lay there, my head spun with thoughts. Morning came all too quickly – the ride to the airport and the flight home were very, very paranoid experiences, almost laughably. I could now cross cocaine and shrooms off the list as experienced more than once and never again. And yet again, they didn't give me the answers I was seeking. I was still on the search for the meaning of life while trying to mentally escape my reality. I wish I could have slapped myself with a stick and said, "Girl! Jesus is literally waiting for you. LIFE is waiting for you…ya big ding dong!"

At around age thirteen, I distinctly remember adopting this weird philosophy that I was going to try every drug. I'm not sure how you just decide that, but I don't pretend to understand all the things "B.C. (Before Christ) Tori" did! I was, and still am, fascinated by them and how they affect the brain. I wish I had turned my interest into pursuing drug counseling instead back then, but you don't know what you don't know. From all the stories I had heard, they "changed your perspective" and helped you "realize things you didn't before." The devil took that train of thought and put action behind it because it was always too easy to pursue finding anything I wanted to try. I even dated a few dealers, and because of my skewed vision at that time, I thought those guys were somehow mysterious and interesting. Satan deviously put people in my path who, unfortunately, provided me with harder drugs. It gives true perspective to "if you go looking for trouble, you'll find it." Man, I kept finding it! Or, it kept finding me! I truly think it was both.

While living with my Aunt one particular time, she said to me, "Sin will take you farther than you ever thought you could go." I didn't get it at the time she said it, but when I hit rock bottom, it kept replaying on a loop in my head. She was right, and I was living it. Satan had swindled me into a lie that manifested at thirteen years old. It perpetuated, and he sent people along the way to aid in the sin which I gave in to. It was the perfect storm. I became someone who then perpetuated sin onto others, encouraging drug use and even being the hands that gave it to them. It's disappointing to know you participated in sin. But that's just it...*sin takes you farther than you ever thought you could go*, and then you look up from it just long enough to realize what a mess you've given in to. And hopefully, you get good and mad. Mad enough to know there's evil at play. An enemy that's very real.

"The thief comes only to steal and kill and destroy. I came that they may have life and have it abundantly" (John 10:10).

Sitting in my sin, now keenly aware of where drug use had *truly* rooted from, I knew it was spiritual, that there was something I couldn't understand or explain at play. I knew it was bigger than the need to disassociate with reality because my circumstances were hard. No, it was much bigger than that! But at that time, since I couldn't put into words what I didn't yet understand, I sat in a confusing state of acknowledging that it wasn't good to continue self-medicating while continuing to use because I didn't know how to stop. It made me mad that I had allowed it to happen over and over, but I didn't know how to address the enemy yet and take back my life. I wanted to fight for my life, a true abundant life in Jesus, but I didn't know how to reach out and grab it.

Plot Twist

While in Houston a couple of weeks later, I woke up on the couch one morning to find Dad sitting over me on the living room coffee table. I sat up, startled, and asked him what was up. Between long stretches of silence, he kept stumbling, trying to get words out. I searched his face for some emotion, but his face was blank. He finally said, "Tori…your mom cleaned out my bank accounts and wants a divorce; we need to get you home." He was so melancholy about it that I laughed a little bit; I didn't know if I should take him seriously. I was waiting for him to say, "Ha! Gotcha!" He didn't, and I started to try and come up with reasons why it could have been happening.

Did she find someone else? Did she join a cult with Cindy? I needed a bit more information from Dad, but he got up without saying much else. I'm not sure if there was any further information he even knew to tell me at that time. Maybe he was protecting me from knowing more. I woke up a little bit more, processed what he'd said, and it hit me like a ton of bricks. As soon as I could collect my thoughts, I called Lex, Derek, and a couple of other friends, and I was on a flight home within a day. It was so quick, I remember sitting on the plane trying to process what the next steps could possibly be. What would happen to me now? Who would I live with now? I brought everything back with me, assuming I wouldn't be back in Texas anytime soon.

I ended up at my Grandma's house when I arrived back in Michigan. No one knew where my mom went, and no one could reach her. All we knew was that she didn't want to be found. We went to the house the next day to see what she had left, and we walked into a nearly empty home. Everything was gone except for some silverware, a small couch, and a lamp. My room was untouched, as well as the bed in their bedroom. I was sure the particular things that she left were to make a statement of some sort. Especially my room, being the only room that didn't have one thing out of place since the last time I'd been in it. It felt like a metaphorical middle finger, reminding me that she was leaving me and my stuff behind for good.

I was so in shock that I could barely utter a word for a couple of days. I couldn't begin to process things when I didn't have enough information about what was happening. No one really knew what was happening or why, not even Dad. He flew back to Michigan a few days later and stayed for a week to attempt to find out where she fled to and hash out anything left with their marriage. She had disappeared and was unreachable. I was staying at the house with Dad the following week, and more paperwork regarding the divorce was dropped off to the front door. I had never seen him so speechless and disheartened. Metaphorically, it was as if a light turned off inside of him, like he hadn't believed the divorce was truly going to happen until that moment.

He flew back to Texas to work after that week, and I'm sure he hoped things would blow over with time and that Mom would reappear. Unfortunately, months passed, and there were whispers but no concrete word on where she went. I was living in limbo between my Aunt and Uncle's home and my house for a good three months.

I surrounded myself with people for those few months, seeing a few different groups of friends in during the day and surrounding myself with all my closest people at night. I stayed high for a while, but then I couldn't medicate anymore – I *had* to feel what was happening in my life. The divorce felt too severe to medicate through, which sounds opposite of what you would think most people would do. I knew I had to be mentally present to process everything. Instead, and only in hindsight, I realized that I surrounded myself with friends all day and all night just so that I could be distracted at all times. I didn't want to have to think about everything that had happened in that house – everything that was happening in all aspects with our family. I had gone from couch-surfing with no steady place to lay my head at night, barely allowed to be at home, to living in my family home by myself with essentially no rules. It was a complete one-eighty, and the most uncomfortable situation. It was so weird to be in the house where so much negativity had transpired over the years, but on the flip side, a bit of an "in your face" to my mom. She had barely allowed my presence in that house for five years, and the tables turned literally overnight: it now felt like my house. I felt responsible to clean it, mow the yard, and in the midst of that, process the fact that I was even there. Life was whipping by my face, and I couldn't keep up with all the trauma and constantly switching gears at the drop of a hat.

Sitting in the Trauma + Why It's Imperative to Healing

I had to process years and years of hurt while living back in the same space that had brought me so much hurt, and it was actually the best thing for me. At first, it felt detrimental, sifting through things in that space; flashbacks and memories flooded in, and I was forced to think about how they made me feel, and why. I was thankful to have the option to sleep at my Aunt and Uncle's when I couldn't stand to be inside those walls for another minute. It had to be done incrementally. Ultimately, it was God-ordained to be allowed to process slowly, at my own pace, with the choice of staying there or with family. I one thousand percent know that it jump-started my trauma-healing process. God created space for me to face things, process, and allow myself to feel again with no desire to medicate, and no desperation to run. For the first time in a very, very long time, I was okay with sitting in the muck of it all.

I thought I was impenetrably strong up until that point. Within the healing and acknowledging process, the iron gates of my heart started to soften. I began having severe panic attacks as a result of having no ever-living clue how to cope with all of these traumas that were coming to light, begging to be dealt with. I got slapped in the face with recognition that I had no coping skills without drugs and alcohol. It became so weird for me to try and figure out how to hang out with friends without feeling like I was going to have an arbitrary attack. Whenever I explained myself to a friend, they looked at me like I had three heads because it was so out of character for me to be anything but calm, cool, and fun. I started to stay home more, although I was never alone. I even had two friends stay with me for almost the entire three months of living there! I couldn't be alone because I was too afraid that a lack of distraction would mean playing whack-a-mole with panic attacks. God was pushing me to face reality! I could feel it, but all I knew how to do with my life was run. He was teaching me how to fight for my life the proper way, not run from it.

One of those nights, surrounded by friends in the living room, my head began to swirl with events. Those memories turned into emotions, which then tornado-ed into panic within minutes. At a loss and trying to keep my cool, I picked up the Bible, arbitrarily flipped it open to Habakkuk, and began reading – anything to take my mind off the intense emotions that were welling up through the tears I was trying to contain.

If you've never read Habakkuk, it starts off with *a lot* of random tribe names, and it didn't make an ounce of sense to me at the time. I might as well have been reading another language! Even so, it was the only thing that calmed me down. Almost instantaneously, it calmed my spirit and gave me peace! I was slightly uncomfortable by how quickly it had happened, all from reading words I didn't even understand. I recall looking straight forward, I could feel my eyes big with shock from the feeling of peace that had washed over my entire body. That's when I knew there was merit to this whole "Jesus thing" again. The presence of God was palpable, and I couldn't deny it!

Stacking Distractions + a Lesson in Who You Allow Close

I found myself in Grand Rapids a lot to visit my cousin, which was meant to be a good thing, but ended up being another space for me to continue running, both mentally and physically. I prolonged facing things and kept trying to bury everything I needed to confront. I had given up on pursuing a relationship with Derek. He was immature and bounced from girl to girl, so naturally, I stepped away.

I met Jake through my cousin on a weekend visit. He was quite a bit older than I, which instantly intrigued me. I was eager for a mature relationship and thought that older meant mature. He was witty, charming, and had a way of giving me his complete, undivided attention like I was the only person in the world, which I was so desperate for. It was an obtuse, unhealthy connection right from the beginning. We were very open with each other that we were also dating other people, but wanting to hang out without slapping any labels on. We were both dealing with emotional fires that we were trying to put out with anything other than Jesus. We became more and more involved with one another, and he ended up staying at my house with me for about two weeks. I figured, why not? I already had two friends living with me; what was one more?

Which, my gosh, looking back, I basically allowed a dude I barely knew to stay with me! That's how much I wanted camaraderie with someone who had also experienced a lot of pain. Or I should say, I was seeking a romantic relationship to latch onto someone who could resonate with me. In reality, it was trauma bonding because neither of us were healed from our hurts. He was basically a stranger. Living with someone before marriage was not how I rolled, it wasn't how I was raised. I was unsettled about it, but pushed those thoughts down because I was too afraid to be alone. I basically had people subconsciously scheduled for every moment of the day to be around me so that I could continue staying distracted from what was really happening.

Like me, Jake was struggling with anxiety and panic attacks, and we both needed someone around who could understand when anxiety hit. I was casually dating four other guys at the same time, all of them older than me. I meshed with their maturity levels much more than the guys who were my age. Derek somehow fell to the back burner, I don't think he could wrap his brain around how much I was going through. Every guy I dated and invested in was just another distraction to add to the pile. I'm telling you, I could not stand the thought of being left alone with my own thoughts! My circumstances were looming and crowding in on me. It was only a matter of time before they would catch up, and I knew it – I just thought I could run faster and further.

My guard was all the way down, and maybe for the first time, because of how vulnerable I was at that time. It's hard to put on a happy face in the midst of a panic attack. I allowed Jake into the places I hadn't shown most people. I believe in being vulnerable with people, but not baring your soul. I believe in being cautious about how many cards I show someone. I bared my soul to this guy who was pretty much a stranger out of exhaustion and desperation. I hadn't rested in what felt like years! I don't mean a physical rest, but a *mental rest*. I needed rest for my soul. Thinking that I would find it in Jake, I showed him all of my cards.

Come to find out a month in, he was married. He had lied to me and told me that they were divorced! On top of that, he had two kids he hadn't told me about! When you bare your soul to someone, things that should only be shared in marriage or an extremely long-term relationship, you create a different kind of connection. He reciprocated his feelings towards me by revealing the truth and laying all of *his* cards out. That turned out to be in my favor because, thankfully, I found out that he had an entire family, and I could get out before things went any further!

I told him he needed to leave the next morning, and just like that, he was gone, and I never heard from him again. Within twenty-four hours, I had learned several lessons about how not to have your life temporarily turn into a *Jerry Springer* episode. I was shocked and angry at myself for allowing someone to get so close, and even more that I had allowed the wrong person in. How had I gotten swindled like that? I was usually so aware of people's intentions and whether they were lying to me or not. I had to forgive myself for meddling in a marriage that I had no idea about, and then forgive him. I felt sick for his wife and family. I knew that if he had lied to me, there were most likely other women he was lying to. It also added to my family trauma in an odd way during that time – not only had I accumulated a bag full of hurt from my own family, my parents were in the midst of a divorce, and I had unknowingly been in a relationship with a man who was deceiving his own family. The devil is busy. I had never been that reckless in a relationship before, and although I was extremely vulnerable, I put some necessary walls back up with every guy I dated from that point on! It was a valuable lesson learned.

People Can't Fill The Voids That Only Jesus Can

I didn't know how to go about relationships or friendships because I didn't have a clue how. I had too many expectations of people filling in all the gaps of pain I had. I thought if I just filled every gap with people with the right answers and love, it would somehow all add up to wholeness. Seeking affirmation from a relationship or friendship where I wasn't the only one with trauma became a full-time job! I needed a lifeline-type of friend, one who would grab my shoulders and say, "Girl, you will *never* find satisfaction for your soul in a man, let alone people in general!" I needed someone to direct me to the answers on how to have relationships. So, here I am as your lifeline friend. If I could, I would grab your shoulders, look you in the eyes, and say: There's no man or human being alive who can heal the hurt you have from other people – only Jesus has the forgiveness Kool-Aid that will quench the need for healing that you so desperately desire. Only He has the map for navigating any and all relationships in our lives!

People will fail you. They'll trample your expectations and disappoint you. No matter who they are or how perfect they've seemed, there will come a time when they will hurt you, intentionally or unintentionally. But guess who won't? God can't hurt you, and He never will.

We're meant for relationships, but as an extension of our relationship with our Creator. We have Jesus as an example of what a relationship – friendships, *and* romance – with other humans is supposed to look like. If we don't have the answers from His word to understand the true way He intended what those relationships to look like, they'll always be peppered with confusion and usually end up being short-term. Why? Because Jesus should be our number one relationship. He was always intended to be in first place, always. Secondly, all relationships require forgiveness, and Jesus is the author of forgiveness! Forgiveness is key for any long-term, healthy relationship, no matter what kind! This world tells us to cancel someone if they've wronged us, or if we disagree with them; Jesus says, "Be kind and compassionate to one another, forgiving each other, just as in Christ God forgave you" (Ephesians 4:32). He also says that we're to make room for each other's shortcomings because they're *inevitable*. "Make allowance for each other's faults, and forgive anyone who offends you. Remember, the Lord forgave you, so you *must* forgive others." (Colossians 3:13). Notice He didn't ask, He said we *must* forgive others. It's required, but it's also what's best for us. God knows that when we forgive, we keep our relationships healthy. If we don't choose to forgive, it turns into bitterness and eventually rots inside of us, infecting every area of our lives in due time. The ironic part is, withholding forgiveness doesn't hurt the other person at all like we wish it did! It disintegrates the relationship, and we have no one else to blame but ourselves because it all started with the choice to forgive.

There's no magic recipe for the perfect marriage or friendship except for the instructions from God. What is God's version of love? The creator of love, *love Himself,* tells us what it should look like!

"Love is patient and kind; love does not envy or boast; it is not arrogant or rude. It does not insist on its own way; it is not irritable or resentful; it does not rejoice at wrongdoing, but rejoices with the truth. Love bears all things, believes all things, hopes all things, endures all things.

Love never ends" (1 Corinthians 13:4-8).

I have this verse on a piece of art, intentionally placed next to my bedroom. This rolls through my brain and is directly in front of me to read when it's a rough day with my husband. It brings those seemingly huge arguments into perspective. Most things aren't even worth the frustration in the grand scheme of things, so I submit it to God's truth first. Then I can gently correct the behavior, whether it's mine or his, forgive or ask for forgiveness, and keep it moving. Your flesh will sometimes hate doing this, mine does too! Don't let the enemy get his foot in it. Roots of bitterness can grow too quickly! Ephesians 4:26-27 says it best: "In your anger do not sin: Do not let the sun go down while you are still angry, and *do not give the devil a foothold.*" Bitterness isn't worth the trade for the erosion of your relationships.

But what about abuse? Some of you might be thinking, "Ok, that's great and all, but you don't know how this person in my life has, and continues to, hurt me." Abuse, whether mental, spiritual, emotional, or physical, should be a dealbreaker. *You're protecting yourself.* I have two scriptures that personally solidify this for me, and I've used them as a map for those painful relationships in my own life.

"Warn a divisive person once, and then warn them a second time. After that, have nothing to do with them. You may be sure that such people are warped and sinful; they are self-condemned" (Titus 3:10-11).

In other words, ain't nobody got time for that, exit left please, and I'll be praying for you! Get to a place where you are at peace with that. Continue praying for them privately until it turns into prayer from a genuine place of love. I've done this. I've started out grumbling through praying for someone who's hurt me, and by the time I've practiced it enough times, it's become a reflex. God transforms my anger towards them into mercy and genuine love. There's a reason that we are called to pray for our enemies. You can feel God's peace when you surrender your enemies to Him, which is what we're intended to do! (Matthew 5:44).

What's The Fruit?

"The thief comes only to steal and kill and destroy. I came that they may have life and have it abundantly" (John 10:10). I won't allow myself to continue to be affected by abusive, hurtful people because it's a paralyzing distraction from living my life with abundant joy. I *choose* to live life abundantly, and that includes the kind removal of hurtful people, whether that be temporary removal because *people do change,* or long-term because I haven't seen the fruit of change in them. God actually tells us to seek out these fruits of change in people and warns us of "false fruit."

"Beware of false prophets, who come to you in sheep's clothing, but inwardly they are ravenous wolves. *You will know them by their fruits*. Do men gather grapes from thornbushes or figs from thistles? Even so, every good tree bears good fruit, but a bad tree bears bad fruit. A good tree cannot bear bad fruit, nor *can* a bad tree bear good fruit. Every tree that does not bear good fruit is cut down and thrown into the fire. Therefore, by their fruits you will know them" (Matthew 7:15-20, emphasis mine).

God gives us evidence of "fruit" or character traits that pour out of people when they're living with His Holy Spirit. I have the fruits of the Spirit tattooed on my wrist as a reminder to live them out myself. "But the fruit of the Spirit is love, joy, peace, patience, kindness, goodness, faithfulness, gentleness, self-control..." (Galatians 5:22-23).

What kind of fruit is the person you're considering letting back into your life producing? I've had family who I love, but they're not safe emotionally for me to be around, so I fervently distance myself from them. It doesn't mean I don't love them, but some people will never be able to hear that they're wrong or that they could have hurt someone else. Pray for them. Pray for wisdom and understanding for yourself to deal with them, too. Ask the Holy Spirit to guide your every word when you have to be in contact with them. Try not to cuss them out or let it crush your spirit in the process! God is your lifeline for navigating every step. "The Holy Spirit will give you the words to say at the moment when you need them"(Luke 12:12).

People aren't perfect – no one has good fruit pouring out of every moment of their life, but it should be consistent! When life presses down hard, I'm paying attention to what fruit is being squeezed out of the relationships around me. If it's bad, I have grace, because sometimes life gets the best of us. But if it's *always* bad character, I'm going to start taking steps back. Only time reveals someone's true character, motives, and the fruits of their life.

God's Patience and Goodbyes

After about two and a half months of living at my house, in the middle of my parents' divorce, Dad let me know that it was time to sell the house. He was trying to sell it while he was in Texas, so there were periodic showings while I was living in it. After another couple of weeks, the furniture in my room needed to be removed. I would hang out with friends or be out late at bonfires and wander aimlessly afterwards – the anxieties of my world at that time kept me up at night and it forced me to be by myself and process. I also needed to recognize how much I'd shoved down still. It was a slow process, because I was only alone without the distraction of people late at night. God knew what I was doing though. He knew my pattern of running and it became more and more difficult to sleep at night – He was creating time and space for me to work through things. It's kind of funny in retrospect – God was so much better at the game that I was playing with myself. He cut me off at all sides as gently and patiently as possible. There were nights where it was two in the morning and I was sitting in my car at the beach parking lot, sobbing through things that I hadn't yet acknowledged. I was praying periodically, although I didn't yet fully trust the Lord while I was still developing a relationship with Him. My distrust ran so deep that I wavered with Him for years, and He was still faithful, diligently showing Himself and pursuing me.

I still had the key to the house, so I would drive home those nights and lay on the floor of my empty room, using my sweatshirt as a pillow. I'd lie awake until morning, recounting memories. I knew I didn't have much time left to feel how much I had been forced to miss out on in that house. For two months, I continued to make myself sit in my emotions as often as possible in that environment in order to move forward with releasing the trauma.

In another month, the house had sold. Dad had a wild company mishap in Houston that ended with him losing his job, along with everyone else who had invested into it. He quickly got a different job in Cleveland, and throughout the next couple of weeks, I was again saying my goodbyes to go on yet another adventure in another state. My friend, Christie, was still living with me on and off during those two last weeks, trying to decide if she wanted to live at home or not, and my other friend had moved back home. It was kind of a small college dorm room experience for a hot minute! Just...a little backwards.

I think my friends thought my life was exciting and unpredictable. Being teenagers, they probably thought it was a life without responsibility and a chance to spend the summer living with their party friend and have a good time! I would have probably thought the same. But under the surface, there was an immense weight and responsibility that I was carrying. The weight of trauma that had built up that I was trying to sort through, all while I was living through more of it. I wasn't willing to sacrifice the opportunity to make memories and have fun with my people in that season. Living freely with my friends in the house I grew up in for a few months is unique, slightly strange, and holds some really amazing times with the hometown people I grew up with! I like to think of it as a backwards way of God's redemption. After so much negativity in that home throughout teenagehood, He was gracious enough to allow me to close my time in it on a note that held laughter with friends. How kind is God? Everything has good sprinkled into it.

Helloooo Ohio + Going All In

I had mixed emotions about starting over again, but I was mostly excited about another big city to explore. The night before the drive to Ohio, Derek and I unexpectedly went to our friend's private beach for a bonfire and He surprised me by sharing that he was ready to give us a real shot. The fire, the smell of the beach, and the sound of the waves crashing while Derek held me around the fire felt like the perfect last hurrah, but bittersweet since time was so short. All I could hear was laughter in the background, and I felt so fearless for the future somewhere else. I was thrown for a loop that something had really taken off between Derek and I! Part of it was probably the pressing feeling that I was leaving in a couple days, and he probably got hit in the face with some realizations. He finally stopped putting me on the backburner and decided that now was the time to tell me how he felt about me. He didn't have to say much and neither did I, there wasn't some great profession of love to one another. It was like everything we wanted to say for a long time came out in action as we held each other next to the fire and wished we hadn't waited so long to mutually commit. Timing definitely wasn't in our favor!

Regardless of the distance, we decided we would give the relationship a try. Because...YOLO! When you're eighteen, YOLO (You Only Live Once) is the motto!

The next afternoon, it was time to make the trek to Cleveland. So many sweet goodbyes later, I threw my Lauryn Hill CD in and started on my way by myself. It was all good. My hope for the future felt strong, I had hope in Jesus now, but I hadn't yet fully harnessed it. I just knew I felt different! I was about to reach another stepping stone that inched me closer to the Lord.

A long month later, after trying to sink into life in Cleveland with Dad and the new apartment, I think Derek and I both took a step back to realize what we had really gotten ourselves into. His first weekend visit to Cleveland woke both of us up to the fact that I really didn't live in Michigan anymore. Long distance was no easy feat, so we ended things during that visit. We still acted like we were together, always talking on the phone and making plans like nothing had changed. No matter how much we tried to go our separate ways, there was an invisible magnet that wouldn't allow it. I didn't know it then, but there was some codependence happening there, and God was working on stripping it away so I would become fully dependent on Him instead.

My relationship with God had grown leaps and bounds since picking up a Bible during that first panic attack back in Michigan. I kept reading every time I felt anxiety of any kind coming on, flipping to a random book and finishing the entire thing. I had progressed to starting at the beginning, in Genesis, to finish in Revelation. Enamored with the word and how I felt reading it, I would sit on the couch next to Dad while reading and ask a million questions. As a little girl, he would quote scriptures all the time that are still drilled into my head to this day. He was even my Sunday School teacher for a while, which I loved! I was mystified by how I was feeling despite a lack of understanding of the word. It proved over and over each time I cracked open the Bible, it was the Holy Spirit that was providing that inexplicable joy, peace, and contentment!

A few months of basically being cut off from distractions and totally focused on the Lord, I was eager to get baptized! During a weekend trip back to Michigan, I stopped by the church I grew up in. There was nowhere that meant more to me in my walk with God than there. It's where I grew up whistling Christmas songs and hymns in front of my family and entire church, where I would swing in the back of the Church, singing "Jesus loves me, this I know..." The foundational Bible stories I heard as a kid there will always be near and dear to my heart. It was, and still is, a place where I fondly remember feeling overwhelming love and joy. I couldn't think of a better place to fully dive in head-first and publicly declare that I was both feet in with Jesus! As I walked through the door to meet with Pastor Kurt (who also happened to be my uncle), my heart instantly swelled up with peace. It felt familiar in a happy sense, tinged with sadness, because I wished we had never left that church as a family. I always wondered what would have happened to our family if we had stayed.

Uncle Kurt agreed to baptize me, and I invited my family to witness. It was even more special because some of my family members who had attended the church since I was a kid were still attending and happened to be there the Sunday morning of my baptism. Dad and my brother, Kurt (who is named after my uncle), surrounded me as I stood in the baptism tub. They dipped me back, and when I came up out of the water, I was overtaken by joy! I couldn't help but laugh. My heart and mind were full of a peace that truly transcended understanding! I knew that no matter what happened from that moment on, I would have the safety net of Jesus' arms. What an indescribable comfort. I went to the bathroom to change out of my wet clothes and allowed myself to feel the moment. Tears of uncontainable emotion fell while I stood in the stall, thanking God for how He'd helped me get to where I was. I felt like I was radiating! What a beautiful time in life when you first feel that fire for the Lord and realize what you were created for. It came full circle in two ways – I was recommitting my life to Jesus in the place I last felt His deep presence in my life, and it took me back to having that joy in Jesus that I had had as a child. That perfect joy still hasn't left me! It's only strengthened, changed form, and matured.

"And He said: "Truly I tell you, unless you change and become like little children, you will never enter the kingdom of heaven" (Matthew 18:3).

I felt like a kid again, only better than that! Childlike joy, trust, and peace filled my soul. I was a different person. I was made new!

"Therefore, if anyone is in Christ, the new creation has come: The old has gone, the new is here!" (2 Corinthians 5:17).

I was a new creation in Christ. There are no words to describe the change that had taken place within me!

All Things Revealed

The divorce dragged on at a snail's pace. Almost every scheduled trial back in Michigan was rescheduled or delayed, until October of 2011, when the day finally came. Nervous, with a sprinkle of every other emotion, I walked with confidence through the courthouse doors by myself. I honed in on Dad's face from a distance, and saw that his eyes were swollen. I hadn't noticed until that very moment how things had physically affected him throughout the almost year-long process since the divorce actually began. I walked up the courthouse stairs, and on my left was a long hallway divided by benches. I quickly realized that teams had formed like elementary gym class, with one side being my mom's "team," and the other side of the bench with dad's "team." It felt like a competitive tournament with everyone exchanging looks and glares, whispering to one another under their breath. It was both silly and sad to watch grown adults who were once close put their backs to each other just a few feet apart, acting as if they didn't know one another. I really wanted to go up to all of them with a half-joking pouty face and say, "Does someone need to say they're sorry or sit in the corner and think about what they did?"

In all seriousness though, it was heartbreaking. My mom had Cindy right by her side and a couple of her friends my parents both used to hangout with when I was a kid by her side. Next to my dad was my grandpa and grandma, aunt and uncle, and me. There were some people, like my maternal aunt and a couple of stragglers who came into the courtroom at the last minute, who all intentionally sat in the middle or to the outside as much as they could, I'm guessing to appear as to not take sides. I'm sure they quickly realized that there was an invisible line drawn down the middle of the courtroom. I wondered how many side conversations and gossip had transpired to create such division, not just in my immediate family, but my extended, as well as in their friendships. I shook my head in disbelief that the hurt had run down the line that far and probably even beyond.

The trial lasted from the opening of the courthouse to close, no joke. The judge said he'd never seen anything like it, and the amount of times he shook his head and made faces during the trial from disgust were too many to count. My Dad barely said one word as his lawyer did most of the talking on his behalf, but I don't think he could have gotten much else out, even if he had tried. He looked overcome with sadness, like he might burst into tears or throw up at any moment.

I glanced over at Cindy, who had arrogantly put her arms up over the back of her chair like she thought she had it in the bag. Like all of her efforts of sabotage were about to cross the finish line. She was evidently proud of her work. As my Mom took the stand, my

Dad's lawyer tore into her. She answered with an offended tone almost every time with frustration and anger in her voice. Towards the end of the trial, my Dad's lawyer had asked a question about me and all I remember is that my Mom answered, "Yes, I do think Tori, our daughter, played a part in why our marriage fell apart." Tears filled my eyes, and before I had made a decision to leave, my bodily response was to stand up and run out. I couldn't withstand the lies, or being painted out as the bad guy any longer. I wouldn't sit there and allow her to shift part of the blame of her marriage failing onto me. I kicked my heels off, ran out of the courtroom doors, and kept on running. I ran barefoot for a few miles until I reached the end of the pier where it turned into crashing waves. I fell to my knees, sobbing, trying to take deep breaths. I kept asking God how He could have let all of this happen. I wondered when He would defend me and take me out of the villain seat. When would He avenge me like His word says it will? After crying and pleading with God for a while, I pulled myself together and thought, *You know what? I'm going back there to ask my mom to her face why she's doing this.* I thought I had to have been missing some big explanation that she hadn't shared with me, and I couldn't miss my opportunity to find out. I knew I wasn't to blame. I needed a better answer.

I ran barefoot all the way back from the lake, ripping through my tights, with tears streaming down my face. It probably looked like I'd just gotten off the plane from the show "Survivor," wearing a dress and tights after being in the wild for three months. When I ran into the parking lot, my mom was walking down the courthouse steps, smiling and laughing with flowers in her hand, as if she had just won the Miss America title. That image is forever burned into my memory and still makes me cringe. This wasn't something to celebrate, it was the end of a marriage! I had asked Derek to come and pick me up for support and to get me out of there. Just as we were driving out of the parking lot, Cindy and my mom were walking towards their car. It was the perfect time to confront her. As she walked past the car, I thought, *This is my only chance! If not now, will I ever see her again?* I yelled, "Mom, wait!" as I got out of the car and ran towards them. The first thing I noticed when I got closer to her was how her face had changed so drastically. Her teeth had gotten dark yellow. Her eyes were black (her eyes were always a pretty blueish-green growing up). I actually took a step back when I got a good look at her. There was something deeply spiritually unsound about her presence, and I felt it so strongly that I had to physically step away. I was looking at the toll that her beliefs and choices had led her to. She had participated in so much gossip, lies, and garbage conversation for years that it was evident from the outside. She was wearing it. It was like looking spiritual warfare in the face and seeing what allowing evil to manifest in your soul turns into over time. The condition of her heart had now flipped to the outside of her body.

It was seeing scripture come to life, too – "If the godly give in to the wicked, it's like polluting a fountain or muddying a spring" (Proverbs 25:26). It was such a visible lesson to me. Who was once a kind, funny, and warm mother was now a woman polluted by consecutively poor choices. It wasn't all at once, it was a slow progression. Why hadn't she guarded her heart better to protect not only her, but our family? I had questions and I deserved an explanation. Shaking with anger, I spat the words out, "Why are you doing this to our family?!" She laughed as she said, "What do you mean?" I repeated myself, then she gave me a snarky smile and said, "Someday you'll understand." I shook my head no, realizing that there really wasn't any space to have a conversation, not with Cindy standing right next to her, waiting to combat everything I said and speak on Mom's behalf. They cackled and walked away.

It was one of the hardest days of my life, and so painful to see who my Mom had become. Being by my Dad's side through most of the divorce process, seeing the turmoil and hurt it brought, as well as the damage my Mom did to me, was excruciating. I was also the only one out of my siblings who was there for the trial, which felt like punishment at the time, but in hindsight, was a blessing. Seeing everything up close, especially as an empathetic person, helped me process grief and start moving forward. It was strange to witness the book close on their thirty-two years of marriage, especially to hear and see in detail as much as I did. So many truths were revealed during that trial, and God knew I needed that! I could begin healing from some of that trauma since I'd gotten some big questions answered visibly for myself. He perfectly orchestrated it in such a way that it unfolded both for my good and His glory.

Learning to Fly on my Own

In August, a few months after the courthouse scene, we moved out of the apartment and into a house on the other side of town. I had been visiting Michigan almost every weekend to see Derek, trying to make things work from afar. I needed stability, and to live and have community in one place, but just like Texas, I felt like half of my life was in one state while living in a different one.

Dad had started dating six months after the divorce, too soon for anyone to wrap our heads around. The woman he started dating, Danielle, changed him into someone I couldn't recognize. Their relationship was erratic, and I know he would agree with me, that's why I am sharing so boldly. She had visited for a weekend when they first started dating, and when they got into an argument in front of me that didn't seem like a big deal, she immediately ended things between them and headed for her car. A little too much drama before I even had the chance to finish my morning coffee! I didn't know Danielle very well yet, but what I'd seen of her was enough to make me run in the other direction.

It was important to me to get back home to try and salvage what was left of my relationship with Derek. So after only a couple months of dating Danielle, Dad set up a plan for me to go live with her for a little bit back in Michigan. I didn't feel like there was any other option, and if he persisted dating her even though all the red flags were waving, I figured I needed to get to know her. It was January of 2012 when I moved into her house, just the two of us, while my dad continued to work and live in Cleveland. It wasn't anything unusual for me, having been used to being tossed around from place to place, but it was one of the more uncomfortable living arrangements. They'd only known each other for a short time and here I was, living with this lady I barely knew and didn't trust.

Being nineteen, I wanted my space and my independence, but Danielle was very restrictive while I was under her roof. She essentially tried putting me on a schedule every day, which I thought strange since she didn't really know me. It was only a week before it became scarily apparent to me that something was very off with her. She would get angry about little things, then tack on scripture to justify her actions when they didn't align (what a lesson that was for me to see being a new Christian!). I became uneasy, and started thinking about whether or not it was worth it to live like that. To be in the house of a controlling stranger that gave me closer proximity to my relationship with Derek, or head back to Cleveland? I started to wonder if I'd given Ohio a fair shot. I was ambivalent.

It was the middle of winter in Michigan, the snow storms were in full force and I was driving from Muskegon to Grand Haven almost every night to see Derek. After about two months of living at Danielle's, I couldn't withstand her trying to control me anymore, so I decided to pack it up and go back to Cleveland. As soon as I got back, I made a decision to get a job and an apartment lined up in Grand Haven, in hopes that Derek and I were headed in a more serious direction. I had the possibility of marriage on the brain, and I assumed he was in the same boat. I was determined to make it work! He and I were coming up on ten months of long-distance, and I knew I couldn't continue with it if I didn't move closer. I'm not sure if I moved home out of fear of losing him, or just to feel a sense of familiarity in my hometown. Seeking stability, I needed to live in the same place for a while. I didn't know how to do that! Even though I had naturally lost ties with half of my friends, if not almost all of them, since giving my life to Jesus, I still felt like Michigan was where I needed to be. What I didn't realize until I made the move was that I had an unhealthy dependency on Derek. He was the only constant I felt I had throughout those past five years.

I drove to Michigan for a job interview and got it on the spot, along with an apartment downtown. *I did it, I. Am. Free!* I thought to myself. I took control of my own life again, and stopped allowing anyone else to call the shots. I recognized that I was the only one that had my back, while simultaneously learning how to give everything to the Lord. There were a lot of great, hard lessons I had to learn in that season on my own!

No More Running, No More Forcing

I settled into the new place, started my new job, and everything was peachy keen for a few months. Being so used to moving every couple of months, I was bored. I felt an urgency to run, as real feelings crept in from previous traumas, from rocks that needed to be turned over. I was becoming really unhappy (bored) at work, and knew it wasn't going to work out. To add to that whirlwind, Derek and I started having serious fights that escalated fast. He was quick to end things when things got too heated, which was a painful neon sign that he wasn't going to fight for me. With the very first fight that ended things temporarily, I fell apart like a bad taco. Until then, I hadn't been honest with myself that I was moving back for him. I told myself that it was for me to protect myself mentally from getting hurt. My motives were out of place from the beginning, and it took our tough screaming matches to see it.

God finally spoke to me after a couple months of crying out to Him with tears, asking for answers on what to do. He audibly told me to let go of the relationship! I needed time to even grieve the *thought* of being obedient to that, so I pushed it aside for over a month. In the back of my head, I wondered how much closer I was to the relationship fizzling out into nothing. I was only prolonging hurt for myself and I knew it. There were a few fights towards the end where both of us declared that it was "over," which propelled us into the vicious cycle of never believing it was really over and excusing all the hurtful things we said. Once, after we broke up for the hundredth time, I actually felt relief! It was changing me into someone I didn't like, cussing him out and begging him to be what I wanted him to be. It was a revelational moment, as if someone put a mirror up to my face. We were both out of words to say and out of apologies. We knew there was nothing left, but neither of us knew how to let go. I finally put a stake in the sand. In the midst of sitting with him, explaining why we had to sever the relationship, I felt freedom! I finally obeyed God's command, and there was an immediate joy that accompanied that obedience! I don't think Derek thought it was really done as I walked away, fully finished in my mind and physically exhausted.

God Can Change Your Entire Life in 24 hours + Walking in Obedience

I had totally forgotten that I'd made plans a few days prior to go line-dancing with Caleb, who I'd met at my uncle's church. It was my way of giving myself a deadline for ending things with Derek, and although I thought it probably wouldn't happen… God gave me a push! After ending things with Derek, the moment I walked up the stairs in tears, Caleb texted me, asking if we were still on for hanging out that night. I know for a fact that moment was God's confirmation for my obedience! He was so gracious, patient, and kind to me. He was waiting for me to say yes because He had someone better lined up for me.

I was too curious to pass up going out with him that night. Completely aware of how hasty it may have seemed to break up with someone and go out with a different dude in the same night, I knew it would have been a mistake not to go. I wiped the mascara off my face and headed out the door to go meet him. I had pre-decided that my intentions with him would strictly be friends, because my heart wasn't prepared for anything else. Boy, did God throw me for a loop! We laughed, we sang in the car together, it honestly felt like I'd known him all my life. All that I kept thinking was, *WOW, God, is this what you've had in store for me this whole time? If only I would have walked in obedience sooner!* We sat on the pier for hours talking, went line dancing, then went back to the pier to talk some more. It was the most natural relationship I've ever experienced, almost strange how peaceful it felt – which was how I knew God's finger was on it. We sat underneath the stars with the waves crashing, and shared our ups, downs, and in betweens until morning. God gave me the gift of my best friend, husband, and prayer partner that night! Within twenty-four hours, I had ended a long-term relationship and found my husband. What a life lesson that was for me, that God has blessings upon blessings if I just quit forcing my own hand! His way is better.

Self-Sufficiency + What Real Love Looks Like

Life was pivoting for me while we were dating; I was still navigating becoming financially self-sufficient, but I had no idea how. I started paying all of my own bills at once when I moved back to Michigan without any guidance, so I was knee-deep in grappling with it when I met Caleb. In the midst of working two rotating jobs, I scoured the internet for anything I could find to help me, and landed on the Dave Ramsey envelope system. Praise the Lord for that, it provided some financial organization! We should be so grateful to live in a Google society where we can teach ourselves about almost anything with the swipe of our fingertips. I taught myself *a lot* from my friend Google during those days – a professional Google-er, if you will. There's no excuse these days to say that you can't do something! The free resources of books, podcasts, blogs, and more are just waiting for us…with a grain of salt, of course.

Caleb was consistent in pursuing me, he never wavered. That was one of my favorite things about him when we first started dating. He was going to Engineering school and would alternate with school and work for a co-op system, which put him in two different places every three months. He'd been on this cycle for a few years when he met me, and he had another year and a half left. Since I had just gotten out of a long-distance relationship, I wasn't too keen on diving right back into another one. Somehow, it was more of a challenge with Caleb! We had a deeper connection, so it felt like an even bigger sacrifice to date someone long-distance. We would have Skype dates, peppered with arguments here and there about how I couldn't do it anymore. I was impatient, and everything in me resisted continuing, but I knew Caleb was worth stretching my patience. I knew Caleb was it, and he had already told me I was it for him. More importantly, God had given both of us the same answer. I had never experienced love in the way that Caleb loved me. He always reminded me about the good parts about myself that I couldn't see. He would drive two and a half hours to see me for just six hours before he'd have to be back in school the next morning! He is pure gold, and he always has been.

Walking away from an old, codependent relationship into one that was bursting with life was hard before it was good. It was the first time I boldly stepped out on a limb to do what I heard the Lord audibly ask me to do. It was somewhat of a practice test on hearing God's voice, as well. Without being cognisant of it, I was testing the Lord, which I was never supposed to do (Luke 4:12). Oh my word, did I test it! I put my head and heart in, but my legs were going elsewhere because I wasn't entirely sure if I could trust God yet. Distrust was a recurring theme in my life, which was understandable, given how my family relationships had been. But it was infiltrating my relationship with God, big time. Isn't it wild how we test God without even acknowledging that we are doing it? It can be a knee-jerk reaction. It proves that we are sinful in our nature. We want to do things in our own power, our own way! So with a mindset of what was "half trust," I went on a few dates with other guys in the early stage of mine and Caleb's relationship juuuust to make sure it was really what I wanted and, most importantly, that it was truly from the Lord (Caleb of course knows of this now). Ya gotta kiss a few frogs first to find your prince!

All of the other dates I went on royally sucked, but I had to get them out of my system before I could put both feet in with surrendering to the Lord. It was the first tangible, can't-deny-it-no-matter-how-hard-I-tried example of how God would provide for me. It was also hard proof that He doesn't make mistakes, so next time I didn't need to make sure if what He said was for real! Praise God that He is a heavenly father who *proves* that He gives good gifts and cares for His kids, even though He isn't required to prove anything to us! I want to provide you with scripture on this. Because like myself, I know there are those out there that have some serious trust issues that might create apprehension to fully surrender to Jesus. Hopefully my story can encourage or prevent you from taking a long left turn in a quest to see if you can *truly* trust Him. Keep these in your heart as a reminder that you can one thousand percent trust His provision and guidance!

We can trust Him as we cast our cares on Him and wait for His help:
"Cast your cares on the Lord and he will sustain you; he will never let the righteous be shaken" (Psalm 55:22).

We can rest in assurance that He provides exactly what we need if we rely on Him:
"And my God will supply every need of yours according to his riches in glory in Christ Jesus' (Philippians 4:19).

"Look at the birds of the air; they do not sow or reap or store away in barns, and yet your heavenly Father feeds them. Are you not much more valuable than they?"(Matthew 6:26).

After we ask for what we need, He guards us with peace:
"Do not be anxious about anything, but in everything, by prayer and petition, with thanksgiving, present your requests to God. And the peace of God, which transcends all understanding, will guard your hearts and your minds in Christ Jesus." (Philippians 4:6-7).

We can trust that He has a great future for us:
"For I know the plans I have for you, declares the Lord, plans for welfare and not for evil, to give you a future and a hope" (Jeremiah 29:11).

He protects us when we trust in Him:
"Fear of man will prove to be a snare, but whoever trusts in the Lord is kept safe" (Proverbs 29:25).

He gave us His Holy Spirit to guide us and we can trust where it leads:
"He anointed us, set his seal of ownership on us, and put his Spirit in our hearts as a deposit, guaranteeing what is to come" (2 Corinthians 1:22).

Obedience is required to step forward into the next level. Imagine if I hadn't done what God asked of me at all–I would have been trapped in a relationship that wasn't meant for me, long-term. I had no idea what a Jesus-centered relationship with a guy could be before I met Caleb – he was, and is, a gift from my heavenly Father!

A New 'Step Mom' + A Side of Karma

Sitting at work one day, a text with news of Dad getting married hit me like a freight train. I'd been wrapped up in my own life and didn't think he would jump into another marriage so soon. It had only been six months since his divorce from my mom was finalized. I was furious that he didn't call, but instead sent a short text that said, "I'm getting married tonight, you can come if you want to". I thought, *I'm sorry...if I want to?!* I was sick to my stomach with anger. It clearly wasn't a priority to him whether or not Danielle would be a decent step mom, or what my opinion of her was. It took everything in me to convince myself that it was the right thing to do to show up for the nuptials later that night. I immediately called Caleb to get his perspective and ask if he could be there to support me. Without question, he made the drive for the night to be a much needed sounding board.

It was a very short wedding at the Pastor's house. They said their vows and it was over within twenty minutes. Her kids and I exchanged some looks of discomfort, as if we all wanted to yell "I object!" one after the next, like in the movie *The Wedding Planner*. I wondered if I should pull Dad aside and ask if he really wanted to do this, but it seemed like I blinked, and all of a sudden, I was signing as a witness. Oh man, do I wish I would have protested against that! I know better now that it wouldn't have changed a thing. I got out of there immediately afterwards with a pit in my stomach.

He had just married a woman everyone else knew wasn't right for him...except for him. It was all uncomfortable, but trying to blend families proved to be the biggest hurdle. It was evident that Danielle wasn't interested in including me or my brother in the family functions, and to be honest, I avoided them like the plague. I was angry with my Dad for not trying harder to include us. Every time I would come over and bring Caleb with me, it was as if my Dad had found himself a new family, kids and all. However, things started to unravel quickly. Her true colors started to shine, and I was welcoming karma to come around.

It was evident that she didn't like me, but I wasn't exactly holding up a #1 foam finger for her, either. It was obvious to me and Caleb that things were coming to a head with them, and we weren't sure what my Dad's next steps would be – but I wished I could have stood in the background holding a giant "told ya so" sign. My grandma said to me once, "God is a God of karma." And I was holding to that; I needed Him to make everything right because I couldn't. In the meantime, I knew it was best to steer clear and mind my own business for a while. I didn't want to get hurt anymore by either of them, and I didn't want to touch the drama with a ten-foot pole!

Living on my own was a repetitive wake-up call, in both good ways and tough ways. It was like consistently getting a car air bag to the face while also feeling liberated that I was doing things on my own. Having previously gotten a vehicle-related drug charge due to my mom telling the cops I had weed in my car and traffic tickets, I had lost my license twice. Getting it back both times proved to be a bit of a nightmare. I had no choice but to drive illegally for almost two years to survive. I was going through jobs like water, too, as I could never get enough hours to pay for my sky-high car insurance. Most days, I barely ate because I couldn't afford much for food. After a while, it got bad enough that I had to ask for some help. When I reached out to Danielle and Dad, I was given the cold shoulder. Both of them knew that I had been estranged from my mom for a couple years by that time, yet they had the audacity to ask, "Why don't you just go live with your mom?" With that, I knew my Dad wasn't in a good place. He had mentally checked out, and being a Dad was his last priority. From his careless words to his actions, I had to protect myself from getting hurt any further and needed to cut myself off from both of them. It was somewhat of a nail in the coffin to the harsh reality that ultimately, I had no parents. They certainly didn't act like parents in that season of my life, and they reminded me over and over that they weren't capable of showing up for me. I just had to work harder and figure it out on my own, which in hindsight, ended up teaching me how to fiercely persevere! It was also a lesson that, although a big decision, sometimes cutting off family is the best option to keep ourselves mentally safe.

People are Not Your Enemy, the Enemy himself is

A few months later, Danielle had called Caleb to bash me, spewing lies about my character and more. I was angry with God for allowing the same thing that happened to me with my mom – the rumors, the lies – all of it was happening *again!* I kept thinking, *haven't I been through enough hell with all of these crazy women?! When are you going to fight for me, God?! Why are you allowing this?* I was exhausted from the gossip and couldn't understand why I was being targeted…at least at first. It took me a ridiculously long time to understand that my character being attacked by Cindy, my own mom, or other "mother figures" was actually an attack from the enemy. It affected me for *years*. For quite a while, I didn't recognize that I was charging every older woman for what these three women had done to me! I couldn't fully trust a woman in general and had to relearn a well-rounded version of discernment with them and start from scratch. I stopped saying, "I just don't get along with women," and quit thinking it was just how it was for me. I stepped out of the victim mentality. It wasn't until I forgave those three women from the depths of my heart that I could see that I needed to recalibrate, stop projecting, and release them and every other woman for any current and future hurt.

Gossip makes you and everyone else around you sick. Some people will choose to participate in it, but the smart ones will challenge it for themselves. The best revenge that I could take was to allow vengeance from God on my behalf – I needed to live a life that reflected the Lord by showing good character and defying the lies that had been spread. That's exactly how God tells us to deal with our enemies!

"Live such good lives among the pagans that, though they accuse you of doing wrong, they may see your good deeds and glorify God on the day he visits us" (1 Peter 2:12).

"Do not take revenge, my dear friends, but leave room for God's wrath, for it is written: 'It is mine to avenge; I will repay,' says the Lord" (Romans 12:19).

After choosing to live by these truths, I saw God fully avenge me in every aspect over time – even twelve years later! Those people struggled, and I saw God teach them and fight for me better than I ever could have myself. People were apologizing to me for believing things that weren't true, left and right. I was able to see God's hand in developing new, fresh relationships from the exact relationships those three women tried to sabotage. He redeemed them! People need time to see concrete truths revealed. Renewal and trust don't happen overnight, even when the ruins of those relationships weren't my own doing. Although it wasn't fair that a negative spin on my reputation was exacerbated, or that they attempted to hurt me, God used it as a lesson that ultimately brought understanding for me. For my good and His glory, as He promises, again and again!

"You intended to harm me, but God intended it all for good. He brought me to this position so I could save the lives of many people" (Genesis 50:20).

People are not our enemy. Read that again. *People are not your enemy!* The accuser, the devil, is your enemy. People – typically unaware that they're being used by the enemy – have evil pour out of them in different forms when they aren't knowledgeable that they have a choice to either live out of love from God, or evil from Satan. That's why we check the fruit. Is the fruit good or bad? What's within someone is always revealed. People's actions and words are inspired from what's dwelling in their hearts. From there, they *make a choice to act.* We have the power to make that choice once we become Christians. Now that we know better, we can do better. When we came into this world as sinners, we didn't know that there was an option to live outside of sin. When we meet Jesus, we become aware of that sin and choose to put off our old self and the sin that accompanied the old version of ourselves.

"To put off your old self, which belongs to your former manner of life and is corrupt through deceitful desires, and to be renewed in the spirit of your minds, and to put on the new self, created after the likeness of God in true righteousness and holiness" (Ephesians 4: 22-24).

We have a constant choice between living out of righteousness or sin, all day, everyday. Sometimes we slip up. Sometimes we choose sin because we aren't paying close enough attention, or honestly, our human desires get the best of us. I believe this is where a lot of Christians slip up – I think it's where those three women who hurt me slipped. They chose to crack the door open and let in a little slander, allowing malicious thoughts to turn into action. We have to keep our eyes open because it can happen too easily to any of us. Our decisions and what's being cultivated in our hearts comes out, usually towards other people. I think of it like this: an angel on one shoulder, a devil on the other, and we have a choice of which voice we'll choose to listen to. Don't you want to be known for loving others rather than gossip or being cruel? I sure do.

"Be alert and of sober mind. Your enemy the devil prowls around like a roaring lion looking for someone to devour. Resist him, standing firm in the faith" (1 Peter 5: 8-9).

"By this everyone will know that you are my disciples, if you love one another" (John 13:35).

Church Hurt - We All Got It + We're All Sinners In Need Of Grace

Seeing people who call themselves Christians choose sin repeatedly is sobering. It reveals that they're not disciplining themselves or choosing to keep in step with the Holy Spirit; instead, they're consciously choosing to repetitively live out their sinful desires. Maybe you've been hurt by someone who claimed to be a Christian – I know I have. I'm also humble enough to know I've been that Christian in a season of ignorance. We all have moments of ignorance as Jesus' followers because we live in a sinful, crazy world. But we should always be growing more refined in this area, learning from our screw-ups, and growing in righteousness.

Church hurt seems to take root when we – believers or not – see other Christians who aren't aware that sitting on a pedestal and declaring Jesus while giving into their own fleshly desires, doesn't work. It's an oxymoron to the way of Jesus. *We can't be both humble and full of ourselves at the same time.* But, since we're all just human, we can still wield hurt by momentarily choosing to listen to the devil on our shoulder rather than the angel, because we are always fighting against our flesh. The more we practice overcoming it, the easier it gets!

"So I find this law at work: Although I want to do good, evil is right there with me" (Romans 7:21).

I say "church hurt" because the church is the body of Christ. We have *all* been hurt by someone who claims to follow God. My personal favorite are the people who just cussed someone out, but then turn around to post a passive-aggressive scripture to their Facebook. Or, as I've learned by living in the south, they gossip about you and say, "bless your heart" to your face. What a goofy, backwards mess.

We have such a massive responsibility to be carrying the light of Jesus around with us. Do you believe that? Every action and word that comes out of us could be just what someone needed as we're being the hands and feet of God. Or…it could completely make someone turn away from church forever. We hold that much responsibility as Christians. It *is* that serious. Do we exemplify a peek into the abundant life walking with God, or shut them out and add to the pile of their church hurt – which will you choose?

If non-Christians don't know that they can live outside of their sin and live with joy, peace, and hope in the midst of pain because of our example, how can we expect them to want to know how good God is in the midst of life's challenges? We have to first be an extension of God's love to them. Let's do our best to *always* be

His love by seeking the Holy Spirit and ask how to act in every situation so that we, hopefully, don't add to more church hurt for someone. It's not easy, but people are worth it!

Peace out, Party girl; Marriage + Another Step Towards Healing

After the lease on my apartment was up, I had a revelation: That year was the longest I had lived in one place in five years! It was special and symbolic to me for that reason alone, but also because I had proved to myself that I could take care of myself – paying my bills and the whole enchilada at nineteen. God was showing me what stability and some semblance of "normal" felt like. There was peace in trusting that my heavenly Father would provide for all my needs, and dang, did it feel good. It was a different kind of security and confidence. He provided another place for me; I rented out a home with a roomie for another year after that. From the outside looking in at that time, it seemed like I was simply surviving – working as a maid at a ritzy hotel on the lake, hoping to make enough in tips that month to cover rent. But in the midst of what felt like a dead end, it was such a special place, because I was sowing seeds without knowing it.

It was the season where I desperately sought the Lord, where Caleb and I planted our first garden together, where we fought for each other, and where we also got engaged! God never ceases to amaze me in His ability to reveal something beautiful through something hard. That season taught me that in my walk with Christ, no worldly circumstance can tarnish the joy and peace God had placed inside of me. I harnessed the power in Him that I was always meant to live my life with. It was such a beautiful time in life, experiencing the goodness of God everywhere I looked. And it hasn't stopped since!

My roommate I'd been living with liked to party late into the night, and this granny needed peace at night with my sweatpants and books, thank you very much. I knew it was time for a new apartment and to have my own space – I had partied enough from the age of thirteen to nineteen to last the rest of my life, ya girl was tired. I had been wasted for almost every birthday throughout my teens, but for my twenty-first birthday, I was sick with a cold and ended up at a local restaurant with a friend for some hot toddies, then watched my favorite movie and was in bed by eleven. The irony makes me laugh! Most people go out with a bang on their twenty-first, but I swapped my love of booze for an early night with a good friend and a chill sayonara drink. It was basically a funeral for my party years. I was happy to say peace out to the super-wild, party-girl side of myself!

Knowing I needed a space of my own, I found a cute five-hundred-square-foot apartment squished into a downtown building. It was perfect. I didn't expect that later it would eventually become the sweet, tiny space where we would begin our marriage journey! Two people in that little space was laughable, but it still holds some of my favorite memories of smacking the heater to stay warm, and walking out on the rooftop to watch the Christmas Parade.

We were set to get married five months after Caleb proposed. You might be thinking, uh…what's the rush!? We both wanted to stay pure until marriage; let's be real, the longer you wait, the less likely that is to happen. We wanted to be faithful to God in that way, so we felt that getting married as soon as possible was the wisest decision. Plus, we were ready to start our lives together! Why wait when you have found the person for you? We both have old souls. Getting married at twenty-one and twenty-two was no rash decision for either of us – we knew what we were stepping into, and sought out in-depth premarital counseling to cover our bases.

Before marriage, I felt the need to reconcile with my family and turn over a new leaf, if possible. I hadn't seen my Mom but one time in three-and-a-half years. In my head, it was (and still is) as if she was already dead, even though she was still alive. It is *so* strange, but as I went through the pain of their divorce and her basically cutting off all communication with me since I was a teenager, it felt like I had processed her death along with it. She and I hadn't been close or talked much at all since I was thirteen. She felt more like a distant cousin I didn't like and avoided, rather than a mother.

It was Christmas and I had been crying out to God in prayer with frustration about my Mom. I didn't want Danielle at our wedding and I was leaning towards not allowing my mom to be there either. Almost instantly, God told me to go talk with her. I didn't hesitate. I grabbed my phone and dialed, wondering if she would pick up for an unknown number. I was taken off guard when she picked up so quickly. I asked if she would be willing to sit down and talk, which she was eager to do and asked if I wanted to that night.

I reluctantly walked to the local coffee shop in the snow to meet her an hour later. I wanted to be obedient to what God told me to do, but I didn't want to do it so soon! There were years of things that had been bottled up that I wanted to say, and they poured out as soon as I sat down across from her. There were a couple of times in the middle of the conversation where she got up and walked out because she didn't like what I had to say, then a few minutes later she would come back in and sit down again without explanation. She would change the subject and act like she forgot about what we'd just been talking through, which I kept bringing back up. I wasn't going to allow her to get off the hook and ignore me. I was shocked that she didn't start yelling or leave altogether. Knowing how sensitive she always was to my Dad's tone of voice when I was younger, I kept my voice soft and quiet with her. She disagreed with me and would not take any responsibility or acknowledge anything she had ever done, which I somewhat expected and had mentally prepared for. I just needed to say what I needed to, to get it off of my chest, face-to-face. God knew that it was necessary for me to see, in person, that she hadn't yet changed, and to grace me with the opportunity to confront her. It was freeing and healing in more ways than one. We left it at a neutral spot with no real conclusion. If she wasn't willing to acknowledge or apologize for anything, I knew it still needed time.

Our Wedding, Boundaries + An Attempt For Reconciliation

Like most girls, I had dreamed of my wedding since I was a little girl. I envisioned flowers in my hair, a flowy, exquisite dress, and for us to share our vows on the beach, with all of our friends and family present. I always have to remind myself that having a marriage more beautiful than your Wedding Day is the most important thing because mine was nothing like I dreamt it would be. Our day was beautiful and special, yet disappointing. It wasn't the wisest decision for me to think that getting all five of my family members into one room for a family reunion after not doing so for over five years was a good idea. I made the mistake of going against my better judgment. I had hoped that it would somehow bring us together and open a door to reconciliation. On the other hand, I knew better and I wish I would have shielded me and Caleb from the emotional rollercoaster. You could feel the tension and there were things I'm sure all of us wished we could have said, but didn't. There should have been reconciled relationships on some level before having to face each other for that celebration after so much hurt. I never would have envisioned that my family would be so broken, having to be seated at opposite ends of the room on our big day. It broke my heart!

The most memorable thing was, of course, the ceremony; that was the point of the entire day anyway, and it truly was a beautiful thing. It was full of peace and love. People still mention how sweet the ceremony was, and that makes my heart so happy to know the part that really mattered most stuck out to them too.

I hadn't seen or talked to my oldest brother, Jay, for five years by that time. To be honest, I was shocked that he showed up at all, although I was happy he did. We only exchanged a few words at my reception; after five years, I thought there would be more conversation. In fairness, him being the eldest kid and me being the youngest, there was a massive age gap, so we didn't speak much growing up because of that. There wasn't much conversation beyond congratulations. My other brother, Kurt, handled things at the bar, getting so belligerent that by the time he gave his speech, he was four shots of Grey Goose in, with no point of return. His speech went something like, "We love, hope, and pray for these things, but sometimes they just don't work out" – referring to my parents' marriage. I was so livid that I asked my aunt to take the mic away from him! The rest of the night, he downed so many drinks that he lost his keys in the parking lot and I had to help him find them because I always felt responsible to help him. I couldn't believe I was having to do that during my own wedding, but I worried that if I didn't, no one else would be there to help him or prevent him from driving.

I had asked my Dad before the big day to refrain from bringing Danielle. His response was, "If my wife can't come, I can't walk you down the aisle". I was so shocked by his response to my request! Considering everything that had happened and how unkind she was to me, I felt that it was completely reasonable of me to ask, but he gave me an ultimatum instead. I tried calling other family members to see if they would reason with him since they didn't care for Danielle either, but they chose not to get involved. I had no choice but to agree for her to come, otherwise he was leveraging giving me away. It was grossly manipulative. To my surprise, he showed up to my wedding with not only Danielle, but her entire family, who were never invited! We had to set up an entire unplanned table for all of them.

I still managed to focus on the reason for the entire day–the promise that was being made between me and Caleb–but by the end of the night, I asked the bartender for a bottle of wine and a straw! I had been mentally refereeing, trying to keep each member of my immediate family from coming for each other all night, and it had caught up to me. My gosh, did I learn a lot from my entire wedding experience with my family. Immediately afterwards, I shifted my mindset and made a decision to quit tending to other peoples' feelings and issues, especially with family. It wasn't my mess to clean up, and it was never my responsibility to fix. I was never responsible for their behavior or decisions. I had hoped that all five of us being brought together would bring positive conversations, reconciliation, and we would all dance together and sing "Kumbaya." I'm giggling now as I write this because I really thought that that was a genuine possibility! Hey, you can't blame a girl for trying! I learned that I cannot expect maturity from unhealed people. It's true what they say: "hurt people, hurt people."

I love them all. I love them deeply. And I slightly want to punch each of them in the face for making my Wedding Day about themselves, in one way or another. The gist of it is, there were multiple lessons learned on boundaries – or the lack thereof. I also learned that not everyone was where I was on my healing journey. Some people just aren't ready, or willing, to do the hard work it takes to heal. Choosing to cut off bitterness and pride, overlook offenses and forgive was only half of the battle; the other half was working on *my* part in the trauma, addressing *their* part, *choosing* to do it differently than before and stepping out of the "I'm right" bubble. It required humility in heaps and bounds along with major new boundaries established. I was only knee-deep into my healing from family trauma and our wedding experience made me see that I still had some work to do to heal. To be the best version of myself, who God created me to be, I needed to separate from people who didn't have my best interest in mind, even from my family.

Shortly after our wedding, I got a call from Dad one night after not talking for a few months – things had ended between him and Danielle. Their marriage lasted a little over a year, and I think we were all happy to see them get off the rollercoaster. He would agree now that it was a lesson learned for him as well. Caleb and I minded our own business and stayed out of the details of their split as much as possible. God is a God of karma.

Seventy-Seven Times - The Opposite of Society

I didn't realize it until the first three months of marriage, but I didn't have someone in my formative years who exemplified apologizing or forgiveness in relationships. I had to start from the ground up with Caleb by practicing going against my sinful nature to always be right (we all have!). Even when apologizing physically pained me, it was and still is worth it. It can be so hard to do! Not only are we fighting our flesh, but we're also fighting what we've been taught by society about all relationships. Society teaches us a self-righteous example that falls short and leaves us in a place of subdued anger. Forgiveness with apologies aren't taught well today, not to mention the layers of pride and insecurity lurking underneath that most people refuse to address because they think it would open up Pandora's box. It might, but it's worth the hard work of addressing hard things in our relationships.

So much of pulling up the weeds to keep the garden of our relationships healthy consists of repeated apologies, forgiveness, and then doing better the next time. The whole doing better the next time part is not a suggestion, it should be a direct product of love and authentic respect for the other person. If there isn't acknowledgement of hurt and an honest conversation about it with changed behavior, our lips were the only thing that committed to forgiveness, and our heart and mind were absent. I read once, "An apology without changed behavior is just manipulation." I think this is mostly true, but I do think that we tend to apologize instinctively sometimes, like an apology on autopilot. Sometimes we just want the argument to end, to salvage the relationship from crumbling any further, to go to bed and quit fighting because we're too tired to hash it out. Sometimes we're afraid to get into the reconciliation process because it feels like there's just *too much* to unpack. We simply can't withstand the possibility of the outcome being a loss of that relationship. Sitting in it to unpack and forgive is worth it though. I'll never stop trying to reconcile the broken relationships within my immediate family – but God has taught me proper boundaries, and in tandem with attempts at reconciliation, they have to be put into practice. I have strong boundaries and deal breakers–they don't have to understand my boundaries, they just have to respect them. I'll revisit the relationship with them after I've distanced myself to see if there's been change when it's spirit-led, and if there's no change or respect, I back away again. Sometimes, permanent distance is the answer, too, but that doesn't mean a lack of love. To me, that's doing my best to live out a seventy seven times forgiveness. I don't always get it right, none of us do, but I keep trying.

"Then Peter came to Jesus and asked, 'Lord, how many times shall I forgive my brother or sister who sins against me? Up to seven times?' Jesus answered, 'I tell you, not seven times, but seventy-seven times.'" (Matthew 18: 21-22)

If I had our Wedding Day to do over, I would elope. It wasn't worth the circus that unfolded. Trying to get my family into one room for just one day where things could be about me and my happiness was a long shot. I knew that before I even started planning, but everyone kept telling me I'd regret it if I didn't have the traditional wedding with all my friends and family. If I could go back and give myself advice at twenty-one, I'd say no one knows you, your family, or your heart better than you! You have to do what's best for you and your newly-forming family – you and your spouse! I wish I would have listened to my instincts, but I'll get my redo one day with a vow renewal, and we'll do things our way. That's the beauty of how God works. He knows the desires of my heart and I know He will fulfill that dream of mine in His own special way.

You, Again?

About two years after I got married, my Mom popped out of the woodwork and wanted a relationship again. With apprehension, my walls immediately went up…but I knew God wanted me to pursue it, to at least give her the opportunity and see if she had changed. A lot can happen to a person over the course of two years. I couldn't figure out why she wanted to pick back up after so long–did she think I forgot that we didn't have any real closure with our last conversation at the coffee shop? With my guard up, I had her over for coffee and we went out for lunch. Once we were out to lunch, the negative talk about my Dad crept in with every topic. I asked that we quit talking about it, but she couldn't. It became clear that this was an attempt to get me to "take sides." To protect myself, I knew I had to cut off the relationship again.

Since that day, It's been almost ten years since I've seen her. There have been minimal sporadic emails here and there that I typically don't answer and we've had one or two phone calls. I have no idea who she is, and if I'm honest, I'm not sure I ever have. I feel like I have these glimpses of who she was. She had this great sense of humor growing up and her infectious laugh could make anyone around her crack up! She always wanted to help other people and make them feel good. And even though she had a light about her, it always seemed like she only gave you half of herself; I was always waiting for the other half. Through conversations with her sister, my aunt, I've come to realize that there was so much that my mom never told me about her childhood or herself. Those things have helped me understand more of why she may have withheld things, but I still wish she would have shared them with me herself so that I could have been more aware and had more of a history and background of her life. I could have known more of who she was. It's taught me to share the fullness of who I am with my kids, though–the good and the bad, the past and the present. It's all important in sharing the fullness of who I am! I want my family and anyone who knows me to get the one hundred percent version of me. Anything short of that is to not live life in freedom and fearlessness. I want to teach my kids that there is no part of them to hide.

I haven't had contact with my eldest brother since my Wedding Day. With both him and my mom, they're like a distant memory that increasingly fades with time, although I know they're still alive. It's a really weird thing to try and describe. It's as if I've fully mourned the loss of them and their death, while simultaneously clinging to hope that God will help them to see the choices they've made and want to change. My mom knows that for us to move forward and have a relationship, I would need to see remorse and genuine evidence of a changed heart. Only then could we potentially have a healed and healthy relationship. With my brother, I've reached out and done my part to try and have a conversation in person, but he's changed his last name and cut off everyone in our family for reasons we aren't aware of. The only thing I know for sure is that I trust in God's plan and I'll always stay open to whatever He wants me to do with both of them. I'll love them from a distance, cling to hope, and keep the door cracked open.

God Provides Mentors + Mother Figures

Words will never express the gratitude I have for my Grandma and my Aunt for the little pockets of wisdom they've sewn into my life. Throughout my teenagehood, living with them on and off for small amounts of time, they were mentors and maternal figures to me. Through tears as I write this, I'm so thankful that God placed two women in my family to be pillars of grace and the light of Jesus. I wouldn't be the woman I am today without the time they took on me. The small, quick lessons that may have seemed mindless to them were priceless to me. God specifically placed them at instrumental ages in my life to pick up the slack and fill the empty spaces my mom was unable to fill.

My Grandma taught me how to unabashedly love Jesus, to fiercely pray over the issues of my heart, to apologize *immediately* after you've wronged someone, and to have a servant's heart. It's so funny–I remember one time she was so disappointed in me after I got a driving ticket and she said, "God says that we're to obey the laws of the land in the Bible – whether you agree with the law or not, that's what we're supposed to do!" To this day, I can't even go a mile without my seat belt on because her voice is in my head like a parrot on repeat saying, "Obey the laws of the land!" She has been a spiritual leader for me almost my entire life in bits and pieces, and I only hope that I can be a fraction of the woman that she is. My Aunt taught me how to be bold, confident, go after my dreams, and to take care of myself. Those are all lessons that have been invaluable in my adult life as a woman of God. He had a timely, very specific, plan as to when they would speak into my life. I owe parts of the woman I am today to them!

I know I'm not the only person who's had a mom, or parent, become absent. If no one has told you yet, *I am so, so sorry.* If they left or abandoned you when you needed them, one hundred percent of the time, it has to do with them and their shortcomings, things they may not have known how to share with you, or they haven't even pinpointed what they need to work on in order to be a present parent. *There is nothing wrong with you* that made them choose to exit stage left. We need that constant and supportive parental figure in our lives, and to have to figure it out on our own in ways we were never meant to sucks. For example, having to work harder to undo bad habits or character we may have learned from them, which is so, so important to do! That being said, you are capable of a fulfilling life without a mother, father, or both parents in the traditional sense, but you do need mentors. You need people who you trust to speak into your life and teach you. You may be in the place I was for a long time: the mentality that

I didn't need a mom or dad to influence me, I'd been doing it on my own for a long time. But friend, we do need a hand. We need a hand to help redirect the hurt towards healing, to allow them to help patch the parts of us that we thought would never heal with their gentleness and love. No matter our age, there is an older, wiser person who we can glean advice from. Even if you do have one or both parents present in your life, you should still look for additional mentors to learn from! Here's some great proverbs on that:

"Where there is no guidance, a people falls, but in an abundance of counselors there is safety" (Proverbs 11:14).

"Without counsel plans fail, but with many advisers they succeed" (Proverbs 15:22)

"Listen to advice and accept instruction, that you may gain wisdom in the future. Many are the plans in the mind of a man, but it is the purpose of the Lord that will stand" (Proverbs 19:20-2).

You might be thinking, *okay that's great, but how do I realistically find someone to mentor me?* First, pray for it. Ask God to provide women to be an example to guide you. Seek someone with a humble heart and ask yourself if you respect that person enough to allow them to speak into your life, or if their life reflects the love and character of Jesus. It may even be a therapist! There's somebody for everybody.

I'm gonna go ahead and put it out there for the elders in the church, too - *please, please,* if you can, make yourselves available to us younger people. We need your gentle correction, advice and encouragement. Notice that Proverbs 15:22 says, "with **many** advisers plans succeed." Especially in the world we live in today, we need those little nuggets of wisdom from many of you wise, God-loving peeps!

Go out on a limb! Boldly approach that individual you want to sponge wisdom from. It could change your entire life. The worst they can say is no!

The Ultimate Parent, Provider, and Best Friend

As soon as I made the decision to fully surrender my life to Jesus at nineteen and go all in, it was a critical time of fighting to find my bearings in Christ, to relearn a confidence and security that the world can't offer. That looked like learning His characteristics and trusting in Him to be my ultimate Father, really allowing Him to be everything my parents couldn't be. That started with diving into the Word of God to understand what His character is.

With a Dad being in the middle of the divorce and completely unavailable at that time and a Mom who abandoned me, God truly took the place of both of them. Not only did I have no choice, but it felt natural, like a reflex. He was always supposed to be my guiding force in every situation from the get-go. Should my parents have been there for me in better ways and made different choices? Absolutely. But it was never in my control. What I think those seasons taught me was that most parents don't seem to fully comprehend how much their decisions and words affect their children. As a momma myself now, my perspective right from the beginning of parenthood was different because of my experiences. I'm conscious of every word I say, what's on the TV, how I respond to my husband in front of my son, how I carry and talk about myself, the company I keep–all of it has an eventual and imminent effect on my little man.

The reflex of our heart should be to seek what our Maker has for us in each situation, and although I selfishly want my son to come to me for everything , I've learned through my experiences that I first need to teach him to seek and ask God first. I want to raise kids who fully rely on their Creator rather than me! We get them on loan until they prayerfully go off to boldly live out the journey God paves for them.

Through that particular season of feeling abandoned by my parents, I realized that the whole point was to run after God, let Him hold me and show me that I'm worth chasing after. *He is the ultimate parent.* He always, always showed me in ways that only I could understand and know it was Him, I just had to pay attention. I realized that God understood my heart better than anyone else could, by blessing me with the little stuff that only He would know made my heart happy–something as simple as someone bringing me hot cocoa, or blessing me with food when I literally thought I was going to starve because I had no money left on my Bridge Card for the month. It wasn't just things I loved or needed though; God was specific, and in the tiniest of details. For example, not only did He send a friend with hot cocoa, but they came with another gift that spoke to my heart, like a sweet coffee mug. I *love* me a cute coffee mug, it speaks to me! It wasn't just food He provided through someone – it was my *favorite* food. It was a friend who showed up at just the right time when I needed them to take me out and bless me with lunch because I had no food in the fridge. A kind "just because" gift from a friend's mom, or multiple invitations to dinner. You might be noticing a theme and a focus on food because I'm a foodie! Only God could have known the little desires of my heart and provided them one-by-one in a short period of time as if to say, "See? I've got you, I know you and I love you!"

During that time, He showed me repeatedly how much He loves me and it helped me to trust Him to be my number one relationship, to know He would always show up if I continued to pursue Him and know Him, just like any other relationship but better. My parents are only human and can never know me like God does. Most of us are relational and need our people, but trying to fill the deepest relational hole in your soul with a finite human being – a parent, a man, or any other human relationship – is wrong and was never intended to satisfy that deep connection with our Maker. Human relationships are just a small, beautiful slice of our relationship with Him, but they will never fully meet our needs in the way that the one who loves us most does. They were never intended to! God just needed to put me through that season to prove to me why.

"And my God will meet all your needs according to the riches of his glory in Christ Jesus" (Philippians 4:19).

God Takes Marriage Seriously and So Should We

I don't often hear people referring to divorce as "trauma." But listen, anything that rips apart the seams of relationships, or creates polarizing hurt that divides people is straight-up trauma. That's not a normal depiction of how families or relationships should operate, even if society tries to tell us it is. The world we're currently living in likes to paint a picture that marriage is a fun thing you commit to for a while, and then when you get bored, you can peace out. As if at any time, you can renew or switch out your marriage, like a car lease.

While I was doing Wedding Photography, I would get so frustrated seeing the lack of respect some people had for such a serious commitment. Marriage *should* be fun and celebrated, but it should also be taken seriously for the lifelong promise you're making before God and your closest circle of people! Some people have the party of all parties to celebrate it, but if it doesn't work out, they just sign a quick paper. I've even seen quite a few "divorce parties" with cakes and all as if it's something to rejoice about. Nah. God doesn't bend to the world's wacked-out version of revolving marriage doors. His Word is so crystal-clear about marriage. Given, you have two people that want to play in the sandbox together and abide by God's perfect plan when it comes to divorce and marriage as a whole. This should always be a huge discussion pre-vows to know exactly what it will take to practice unconditional love because it's no easy feat!

I'll never forget sitting on the couch in Cleveland one night in the midst of my parents' divorce, and Dad had a moment of expressing how divorce felt in the only way he probably could. With tears in his tired, red eyes and a sharp, loud voice, he repeated, "You just don't understand, this is like if someone were to rip one of my arms or my legs off. It's like losing a limb. Like a part of me is dead." My dad isn't emotional and never shared much of anything personal from that entire process with me, so that stuck with me. I think it was the desperation in his voice, like a plea for someone to just make it all stop. It was a real-time, painful result of the fracture of the unity of two people's souls that were never meant to be separated.

"That is why a man leaves his father and mother and is united to his wife, and they become one flesh" (Genesis 2:24).

"So they are no longer two, but one flesh. Therefore what God has joined together, let no one separate" (Matthew 19:6).

It's only natural that an untended marriage will cause trauma if problems are ignored and allowed to fester. This will affect the kids, and possibly even more people, involved. Besides our relationship with Jesus, our marriage is the second most important; if it becomes off-kilter, so does everything else.

I could open up a gigantic box of scriptures and get into a whole journey with you of what Jesus says about marriage and divorce. What I love so much about the Bible is how scandalously direct it is. God doesn't skirt around edges with most things. I would highly encourage you to do a deep dive and find a list of those scriptures, if you're curious. I'll leave this last solid piece of biblical advice from Hebrews 13:4 that feels like the antithesis of our society's ideologies on marriage –

"Marriage should be honored by all, and the marriage bed kept pure, for God will judge the adulterer and all the sexually immoral."

God doesn't play with marriage, divorce, or the seriousness of both. The shrapnel from the bomb of divorce hurts everyone in proximity. Those who surround the people facing divorce are losing lifelong relationships too! They may be mourning memories and feeling like they have to choose sides. It's a heavy burden to bear for everyone involved, and the effects can linger for years.

We Have a Choice To Heal

As it's been over a decade and a half since the divorce, the sum of everything I've learned is that there is truly no greater gift than time. Sometimes years feel like they drag on forever, there's no substitute for it. I've witnessed it propel some families into healing or cause them to fully give up on healing. I myself started to give up until I realized how much the things I hadn't healed from were affecting every relationship that I had, and the way that I perceived people in general. Maybe you have behaviors or patterns in your own life that you've realized are problematic, but you don't know how to correct them. Maybe you know you learned them from your parents, or maybe they're a trauma response from things that have happened to you. No matter the origin, we all have a choice to grab God's hand and say, "Show me what I need to do to heal!" It may sound backwards, but God had to deal with *my* heart first. He had to bring me low and open my eyes so that I could put my pointing finger down and learn to love the very people who traumatized me. Love was the first step to healing and allowing God to get His footing in it and begin working. I don't want to downplay how hard this can be! I still have to ask God to give me His eyes to see people, to help me to love people I don't understand. But with every genuine prayer to love, God gives me a little more of His vision of how He views them. Every time, it heals a little more of the hurt. I implore you to pray the same: choose to heal and start at square one with love. I can't promise the rest is easy, but it's worth every effort.

"Beloved, let us love one another, for love is from God, and whoever loves has been born of God and knows God. Anyone who does not love does not know God, because God is love" (1 John 4:7-8).

"Above all, love each other deeply, because love covers over a multitude of sins" (1 Peter 4:8).

How easy is it to focus on the hurt and wrong that's been done to us, to harbor the apology that would be so simple to say? An apology could create space for new life in a relationship, yet so many of us just aren't ready to release that control to God. We want to change that person and make them aware of how much they've hurt us! Because really, that's what it is. None of the healing change of someone else's heart is in our control, and that can honestly feel annoying, but It feels so much better once we relinquish control to the Lord. We were never meant to heal a heart–only Jesus can do that–we can assist in it, but ultimately, the other person has to choose to surrender their heart and go through the process of dredging up the roots on their own. I've learned the painful lesson that I don't want to be the one to try and force change, because the constant disappointment is like repeatedly getting beat over the head with a bat. *You can't change people, you can only love them.* Loving them best often looks like repeatedly surrendering them back to God. Trying to force someone to just be that "normal" sibling, the parents or family member you wish they could be, or even the friend you need them to be…it just results in anger and disappointment. I got beat with that bat for years before learning that as much as I love someone who I desperately wish would change, as angry as I may be and want them to see how they hurt me, they aren't my responsibility.

I heard something once that sticks with me – "Holding onto anger is like grasping a hot coal with the intent of throwing it at someone else, yet you are the one who gets burned." Doesn't that just hit you in the gut?! There's so much freedom and peace in taking that hot coal of anger and giving it to the Lord. It was never meant to be ours to hold onto in the first place!

The Way We Use Our Voice + Set Boundaries

Proverbs 15:1 states that "A soft answer turns away wrath, but a harsh word stirs up anger." It took a great deal of time for me to learn that I was going to have to live that scripture out with my family more times than I wanted to, particularly in moments where yelling would have been fair on my behalf. Learning to be soft-spoken and calm in the heat of conflict has brought so much healing and peace while navigating difficult conversations with family. I've been shocked by the ability God has given me in those moments to stay level-headed when all I've wanted to do was scream and abandon ship. This doesn't mean that I allow anyone in my family to steamroll me or yell at me: Boundaries don't get put on pause just because it's family.

Have you ever heard someone say, "That's just family, you just have to deal with it!" or something along those lines? I respectfully disagree. By saying that, you're creating space for abuse. That it just "is what it is." To that, I call BS. That's a cop-out on setting boundaries, in my humble opinion. You may have even heard it from a parent, or someone else who hasn't been able to set their own boundaries with family, because they were never taught that you should have them. Boundaries are for *you*. The Bible is chock-full of boundaries! Every single command we're given, every wise verse of scripture, every Proverb, is an instruction manual on a boundary we're supposed to have. Almost all of them are choices and actions that must be done to put that boundary in place. Here's the definition of a boundary:

"A psychological demarcation that protects the integrity of an individual or group or that helps the person or group set realistic limits on participation in a relationship or activity."

Basically, a boundary is something we say or do that keeps us and our relationships in a space of integrity. Our boundaries and our relationships go hand in hand: We set a boundary first for ourselves to protect *our* integrity, and by doing that, we teach the people around us our boundaries, which keeps our relationships in a space of integrity. I think of it kind of like the common phrase we all hear, "You have to love yourself first so that you can love others well." We aren't loving ourselves or others in the best way if we continuously allow someone to steamroll or berate us. Instead, because we are image bearers of Christ, we love others and set boundaries with them as an outpouring result of the love and confidence we receive from Him. Love requires boundaries. Even God has boundaries with us! Have you ever asked Him for something and didn't get a word on it, or what you *really* wanted or needed didn't work out? Or maybe He told you to do something instead of the thing you wanted to do. He puts up boundaries for us as a way of showing His love for us.

We have all had people try to test our boundaries or manipulate them. It took me years to learn how to set them and to boldly sit in them, even repeating myself several times when someone chose not to respect my personal boundary, especially with family! Use your voice well. You don't have to raise your voice, you just have to be specific and kind. I did boundaries backwards for a long time, and I think the majority of our culture has taken to this as well – we tend to *physically* set a boundary before we set the *verbal* one. For example, it's a lot easier to ghost your Auntie Susan instead of having a hard conversation about why what she said last week at that family party really hurt your feelings. In the long run, you just did yourself a massive disservice because you allowed a root of anger or bitterness to start festering between the two of you–ignored and suppressed feelings that should have been verbalized don't just go away. They sit and rot subconsciously and eventually come out in other ways. By having that hard chat with Auntie Susan, you can release bitterness and set a boundary for yourself and that relationship going forward that says that form of treatment won't be tolerated. It also shows love because you value the relationship so much that you're willing to put your emotional cards on the table, not knowing how it will be received. You hope for a normal response, that she acknowledges your feelings with a verbal ask for forgiveness. Then boom! It's over and you can be on your merry way. That's the way it should be!

In today's age, ghosting people has become the norm. It's turned relationships into more of a commodity by discarding people when they cross boundaries that were never even verbally set. People think they can just continue to replace others until they find the perfect person who never hurts them or disrespects their boundaries. I've seen it over and over. And my question is usually, "Well, did you tell them how you felt about that?" and the answer is usually, "No, but they should know better!" People aren't mind readers. Let's quit treating each other like that person should just know that they hurt us, when in reality we didn't even open our mouths to tell them. Someone in church leadership who was mentoring me and my husband once said, "Speak the truth, but do it in love." Paul David Tripp puts it beautifully – "Truth that is not spoken in love ceases to be truth because it is twisted by other human agendas. Love that is not guided by truth ceases to be love because it is divorced from God's agenda."

Paul says it best, though. "Instead, we will speak the truth in love, growing in every way more and more like Christ, who is the head of His body, the church" (Ephesians 4:15).

If we can't set a boundary or speak truth to someone with love, we should sit on it with prayer and sit at Jesus' feet before approaching them. If we can't pour out from a heart posture of love, we have to first work on ourselves before addressing someone else with love that we may not yet possess for them. Remember, boundaries are God's idea!

Turning Over a New Leaf

This is the part of my story where things start to get better for my family and rise with hope, the ongoing turning over of a new leaf. As the reader, I hope you take note of the beautiful progression of seeing God's hand in it all, and how He can work in our hearts and the people close to us. He's just that good…

A couple years after Caleb and I got married and the dust from the whirlwind of both of Dad's divorces started to settle, I got a text from Dad that said he had someone he wanted us to meet. I'll admit, the first thought that sailed through my brain was, "oh boy…here we go again, wife numero tres." Not to be a Negative Nancy, but you can understand why I felt that way; with the way the cookie crumbled with Danielle and the second divorce, I had severed myself from my Dad's life almost completely. Caleb and I had him over a couple of times to catch up during that gap of time where he was single, but being pulled into his marital life wasn't healthy for us. In that instance, ignorance was bliss! I'd grown in setting boundaries by then and had a different perspective regarding family altogether.

We went out for dinner to meet this woman, and part of me wanted to pull her aside and be like, *homegirl, I know I don't know you but...the last two weren't exactly worth repeating. Do some digging and make sure you want to take all of this on!* Another part of me was numb to it and didn't really care to be involved whatsoever. Even after having to make the choice of cutting my Dad off for quite a while, I was still protective of him and cared deeply about him. Before getting to know Jane, I wondered how many wives he would go through before finding one that wasn't crazy with a capital C. My walls were understandably sky-high, but something did feel different about her. She was warm, funny, unabashedly herself, and very transparent. I could sense that she was genuine and also treading lightly herself. She seemed to be aware of what she was walking into, and she was fully expecting us to be guarded. That sparked hope that my Dad had begun the relationship with honesty. I was quiet, observant, and suspicious.

As it turned out, the more we wandered through conversation, we found out that they had been dating for a long time! He was having us meet her to get our take since he was planning to propose a week from then. After they were engaged, they asked me to photograph their wedding, which was admittedly a little awkward. I treated it like I would a client since in the back of my head, I still wondered if it was too fast and we weren't sure if she would flip on us all at some point like the last two had. Even so, I didn't have the same expectations this time around. I wasn't hopeful of her becoming like a mother to me or replacing my mom in any way. I didn't know what to expect, which in hindsight allowed space for God to make it something new! On their Wedding Day, I felt immense joy for them, especially Dad, but I still had reservations and kept my distance emotionally. Jane grabbed me, looked me in the eyes and said, "Tori, I'm going to take care of your Dad, I promise. I mean that." Even now, with tears in my eyes, I remember feeling the brick wall I had previously put up to protect myself come down a bit. It was a small, first conversational step towards trust and I could feel that she meant it. I could let go of the protectiveness that had been built in my dad's defense from the past two women who I had expected more from. She turned around, and I smiled to myself and thought, "Yep..this one's gonna be different!"

The Gift of Time

Someone said to me once, "You spell a relationship, T-I-M-E." Time. Man, I wish we understood that more as humans. Needing to still reconcile some things at that time with Dad, I was intentional about having hard conversations with him in an effort to have a father-daughter relationship with an open door. I was patient in giving it prayer and time. The next year at Christmas, I was completely caught off guard by a gift from him that was better than any gift in a box–an apology. He apologized for the way he handled my wedding, the way he handled things with Danielle, and verbally recognized that I deserved better than that. I was crying, Jane was crying, even my brother was crying! Initially, I wished for an apology that was more than that. My thoughts ping-ponged from one offense to another that he could and should have apologized for, through homelessness and abandonment in my adolescence–then I reeled it in. My Dad had never said sorry to me before. *Never.* What a step it must have been for him to humble himself, to take responsibility for the specific parts he played in the way my wedding unfolded. In that moment, I had to decide if that apology was enough for us to move forward with our relationship. I quickly made a mental note that it was worth celebrating as a stepping stone in our reconciliation. I needed that to fully forgive him for that massive offense; however, there was still more work to be done. There was more to share with him regarding how deeply he had hurt me over the years, and in order for us to have wholeness in our relationship, I knew I would have to open my mouth and say what those things were. Did I want to continue doing that? Of course not. Who wants to dredge up the past and dig for answers? But when you continue to be hurt by someone, it can feel like every forward step you take in a relationship is met with a minefield needing to be defused. I refuse to sweep things under the rug so that I can get the answers I need for my continued healing. By doing this, I'm continually establishing boundaries for myself. I will not allow anyone to repetitively hurt me, or pretend something that hurt me didn't happen, especially if that relationship is important enough to fight for. To fight for the relationship when it's necessary shows that I value it, no matter how hard it can be!

This all takes time. It's been years of practicing this with Dad, as well as in every close relationship in need of healing in my life! And it doesn't look that same with any of them. Sometimes it takes time for God to work on a heart. It could be the perfect scenario and teaching moment that only God knows speaks to that person, ushered in by the right person at the right time with the right heart posture. We have to give God, ourselves, and other people space and time when it comes to healing. He's working on it, even if it feels like it's one small step towards restoration at a time.

Doing Our Part in Healing - Apologies + Hard Conversations

Remember Xanga? It was one of the first social media, blogging platforms. I'm laughing to myself now. I started writing my testimony on Xanga while sitting in our little apartment in Cleveland in 2011. I didn't understand why, I just knew I had to write it down. Since then, I've rewritten it several times. I've added to it as hard things and refinement have shaped me throughout the tail end of healing from traumas. About a year after the pivotal apology from my Dad, God told me to share my testimony I'd written with him. I still remember where I was when He told me, along with the face I made in reluctance. I remember saying, "No way God! He's not going to care about this!" I drug my feet in obedience. On a visit back to Michigan, I printed out all the pages I had written, put them on the chair in front of him and said, "You need to read this." To my surprise, he agreed. For the next three hours, he skimmed it and we talked about it at the kitchen table. He agreed with some of it, dismissed or disagreed with the rest. Ultimately though, it was most important to me that he acknowledged at least some of the hurt that he had caused and how we had ended up in the place that we were in our relationship. I *had* to have that if we were to keep moving forward. I required it. Did I get all the apologies and acknowledgements I was hoping for from him? No. But they were enough to continue creaking the door open a little further in the process of restoration between us. He was willing to put in the time, and that was what I needed to see.

Never underestimate the power of an apology, even if it's years later. It's not the original way God designed it because we're called to say that we're sorry and ask for forgiveness right away before things get messier, but God can bring healing at any time if we're willing to humble ourselves and let Him guide us!

I think those closest to me might describe me as somewhat confrontational. I suppose that may be true, but hear me out. First of all, there is so much scripture that supports bringing up hard things with people! We aren't called to sit back and swallow our words all of the time. Granted, the Holy Spirit should ultimately give us guidance as to whether or not we speak up. All of these lead us into action in our relationships:

"The Holy Spirit will give you the words to say at the moment when you need them" (Luke 12:12).

"If another believer sins against you, go privately and point out the offense. If the other person listens and confesses it, you have won that person back" (Matthew 18:15).

"Bear with each other and forgive one another if any of you has a grievance against someone. Forgive as the Lord forgave you" (Colossians 3:13).

There's something to be said about having a disagreement between a believer and a non-believer in general, but especially when it comes to family because we're taught that "we can't choose our family." We have higher expectations that we should just accept them and move on, apology or not. If they're a Christian, they know the calling we have of stepping outside of our fleshly thoughts and desires to be right with bringing up offenses. They often have a different willingness to forgive and move on. They should respond with love. I think that's important to hang onto and remember when approaching someone to resolve something. Are they Christians and are therefore open to gracefully hash things out with love? Do you yourself have something to apologize for? Could the offense be easily shut down with a dose of humility?

Maybe this time you go first. Get that hard thing out in the open that you've been carrying between you and a family member or close friend for months or years. God is for your family, healthy relationships, and for reconciliation. Satan is not for your family. It's time we fight back with love, dig up the roots and keep the relationship growing upwards. Will you fight for your family or relationships when it's hardest to open up your mouth and have that hard conversation that could lead to a fresh start? It's time. Rip off the Band-Aid. Once you do it, you open the door to make it safe to do again until it becomes a regular routine to get it out and move forward. You might even be surprised by what they've been harboring towards you and may need to ask for forgiveness yourself!

Keeping It Real + Being Exactly Who God Created You to Be

I was dealt a really ugly hand of relational issues with family that looked really pretty and shiny from the outside. With manicured hair, a done-up face, and nice clothes, it's hard to view what's going on in someone's personal life. What no one knew was that I was living on a prayer to survive throughout the majority of my adolescence. And guess what? No one wanted to talk about what was really happening with me. I was swept under a rug or ignored in many cases.

I've never been one to pretend that I have life in the bag by any means, but I've experienced over and over again that people see what they want to on the surface. People are never who you *think* they are, nothing is ever as it seems, and there is always more to the story. Always. People are too complex to be put into a box, so why do we try to? I crave authenticity and transparency in myself and from others. I love that so much about God, that He's the King of authenticity and transparency! I can try to play Him and He will call me out in the most unexpected, sometimes hilarious, ways. He'll speak to me and correct me on something and I'll just sit there and laugh because I knew better. Realness is so important with God, yourself, your friends, family, and even strangers. Practice it. Challenge the social media-ridden world we're living in that tries to tell us that we need to curate a perfect life in squares on the internet. Ask God to help you to be the weird, wonderful individual He created you to be. Be fearlessly authentic wherever you're at and with who you're with in each moment.

I wish I would have had the tools and prayers to ask God to help me be myself with my family in particular when I was young. I had no issue with being myself in front of everyone else! But because of an expectation of perfection, it didn't feel safe with family. I didn't feel the warm welcome of "come as you are." No matter which stage of life I'm in now, God has shown me that that's part of the beauty of who I am. Quirky, little ole me. God has re-taught me how to love myself in all seasons instead of the version of me the world wants me to be. Healthy confidence is not something the world teaches well. We're taught to one-up each other, that we shouldn't reach out too much for fear of appearing too needy, to stay quiet and not speak up for fear of being judged, comparison...the list goes on. I'm still learning how to talk to myself kindly, to *never* talk negatively about myself, and to take time to do things that make me feel alive. The confidence of knowing that I belong to God, that He protects me and is the source of my value is far more comforting than any form of human approval or wordly nod of well done. Every single one of us wants to feel loved and valued. But it must always be rooted in the knowledge that we *already are* by the one who made us. Only then are we immovable when the world rejects us – which as Christians is inevitable. Never stop resting in God's truth of who you are. Speak the beautiful truths of your identity and God's promises over yourself from His word. Look in the mirror every day and remind yourself that you are dearly loved by the one true King and that He dances over you with singing! (Zephaniah 3:17). That's the only true unshakeable confidence that this world can't strip away from us. It's untouchable!

Breaking Off Generation Cycles

I rest assured that the spirit of divorce that unfortunately affected my family, the patterns of my mom's past or the past behaviors that affected her or my family *end with me*. I'm a new creation and woman through Jesus, I have a new bloodline. I don't live in fear of her actions continuing through me because I'm confident that God won't allow that as long as I stay in tune with His plan and obey His course corrections along the way. There IS power in declaring that over my life and *you can and should do the same* if there's been a long-term pattern of addiction, depression, or divorce that's been passed down from generation to generation or any other issues that have overstayed their welcome in your family. God can and will take you above those things if you trust and wholeheartedly depend on Him. That doesn't mean it's easy and you might have to fight harder than those who don't struggle with the above, but understanding that it's a spiritual battle is the beginning of knowing how to combat it.

"For our struggle is not against flesh and blood, but against the rulers, against the authorities, against the powers of this dark world and against the spiritual forces of evil in the heavenly realms" (Ephesians 6:12).

Do you want to cut off those tendencies in you or in your family? To create a new, redemptive path going forward that only God can forge for you? If you do, pray this:

God, _____ (name the issue!) has gripped me and my family for too long. It's been a cycle that I'm tired of being in and of seeing it wreak havoc on me and my family. Father, in the name of Jesus, I cut off all _____ from me, my present family, my children, and my future family. Cover us with your healing blood and create a new generation bloodline in me and my family. Create new life, redemption, and freedom in me and my family! I break off any evil that has attached itself to me and I cast it down to the pit of hell. I replace it with your holiness and your holy spirit. I surrender my life to you, God. Holy Spirit, lead me in everything I think, say, and do. Renew my mind and help me to fight the good fight. I claim that I am a new creation in Christ, your special possession. Place a hedge of protection around me and my family. Go before, behind, and beside me to cut off the enemy in every direction. Your promise is that you will fight for me and that I only need to be still. My heart is yours, and I surrender my family to you. In Jesus' name, Amen!

It Gets Better

I love the song lyrics, "He makes beautiful things out of the dust." I was dust. Before Jesus, I was always hitting a wall, going nowhere fast, and striving towards meaningless things. Maybe you were, too. Maybe you're there now. Life is but a breath and I chose to stop sitting on the sidelines of my life and jump in with both feet. I made a conscious decision to inhale the little blessings God gives me and see the painful moments as stepping stones to wisdom and a deeper connection with Him. I can laugh about the pain of my past with joy for the future and trust in God that He's allowed me to be dragged through the mud for a bigger purpose. I rise up with hope and joy, knowing that He is renewing me and working on me with each new day!

I still get sad when I think about my immediate family being spread all across the US without much contact, and wonder if all of us will ever be together again. Grief comes and goes in waves, and I can really feel that pain in my heart some days. I cry harder than most people do at family-oriented movies (even comedies sometimes!), and on rare occasions, seeing a mother-daughter duo out shopping can make me feel a bit sad because it hurts to lack that relationship. However, I don't sit in shame over it, wallow, or give it much of my time outside of prayer. It's crucial to snap out of it, put my feet on the floor and say, "God, I surrender it all to you." Because the truth is, it isn't my burden to carry.

The hope we have is everything, and I genuinely cling to that and choose to believe the best, that God will do a new thing in my family. Even when it's hard to press into that hope, I can recollect what God already has done. Because I've seen evidence of it! But even with that hope, I recognize full restoration may not happen in my lifetime. It might not happen in your family or relationship either. Instead of viewing it as a burden, I reframe it and see it as a gift. We can't control people or change them; what a gift to lift that responsibility and leave it to the God who knows each of us best. Only He can truly change a heart, not us. We can hold true to the promise and hope that He's doing something, even if we can't see it. It may not be in others, it may be in us!

"See, I am doing a new thing! Now it springs up; do you not perceive it? I am making a way in the wilderness and streams in the wasteland" (Isaiah 43:19).

No matter how much time passes without a relationship or conversation with my mom or brother, I will always treat them with love. I will keep healthy boundaries and leave the door cracked open for them. All of our lives are broken at times and God gives us grace and mercy through the cracks, reminding us that He loves us so much that He won't ever allow us to completely shatter under the weight. He'll glue us back together with love and grace. In the same way, I see the cracks of brokenness in my family as openings for me to be the love of Jesus. Change the way you see brokenness, and it can change your life. Boldly face brokenness, don't run from it. It's in the brokenness that we're faced with the opportunity to desperately fall at His feet to find His peace, presence, and answers. It's by design. What a blessing to have His comfort waiting for us at all times, whenever we need Him.

It's been over fifteen years since enduring trauma all throughout my adolescence. It's been thirteen years since that earth-shattering divorce snowballed through my family. I have done my part to heal, and have seen God work overtime in doing His part. My family isn't my identity. My past isn't my identity. It isn't yours either. The world teaches us that "family is over everything." Family is complicated, whether it's our blood relative or our family by spirit. It's all messy and it all requires sitting at the feet of the one who has the answers to teach us how to deal with them.

Self Awareness + Facing the Trauma

One thing is for sure: We *must* deal with our trauma! If left unresolved, it will rear its ugly head in strange ways that, at first glance, don't look like trauma expressing itself. Let's pay attention to our reactions to things – the way we handle things can be such a huge indicator that there's a deeper issue at heart. There's behavior because we have a bad day or an attitude, then there's repeated behaviors or even illnesses because we haven't dealt with things that have manifested within us. You should be having moments where you're recognizing and differentiating between the two. Where you realize, oh snap, I just acted out of pocket and it wasn't like me - Lord, what is this really about? Help me!

Also, do not sleep on therapy. Getting things out verbally, having someone else's perspective to sort out the pieces with you and make sense of it is *essential*. Sometimes hearing a therapist's acknowledgement and maybe even having them bring awareness to traumas we need to work on is key to identifying the root. Cry, process, and get tangible tools to help you live a better life, to be a better human and show up as the best version of yourself. Don't you want that? I'm a huge proponent that Jesus partnered with therapy is the best combo, so I will always advocate for finding a Christian therapist. And if I may gently say, my friend, the hard work starts with ourselves. Even when we're in the victim seat, it's our responsibility to make moves towards wholeness. Did someone in your life ever say to you, "God helps those who help themselves!"? Did you just roll your eyes? Me too. *But* it's true! There's no coincidence that part of our relationships with other people is them pointing out things within us that need refinement, because that's part of our relationship with God too. Boldly step out in humility *and* respect for yourself and start unpacking your negative behaviors with a therapist. In today's hot mess culture and crazy world that seems to throw things at us left and right, it's a consistent work to keep our heads on straight and fight the good fight of faith. I'm a firm believer that therapy should just be a part of our heart maintenance these days. Show up and advocate for yourself, so in turn, you can be present in this world as the shining, glittering version of you that God intended for you to be.

Every single one of us has trauma, whether rooted in family, childhood, or otherwise, it's in the undertones of our lives. We must dig up the roots to get rid of the bad ones and allow time and prayer to produce new roots within us. Eventually, flower buds start to develop and God begins to do a new thing. The cycle continues. We are never done being pruned and refreshing our soil to have beautiful fresh buds and new fruit appear. We must stay attached to the one who makes all things new, who calls us to be better, who takes us out of trauma, redeems us, and crowns us with love!

"Who redeems your life from the pit and crowns you with love and compassion" (Psalm 103:4).

My gosh, is God kind. Do you remember when you first surrendered your life to Him? (If you haven't, there's a simple prayer on the next page) How refreshed, new, and filled with fire and love for life you were? I do. Let's remember our true identity in Him. The abundant life that He promises us thrives after we are redeemed from the pit of sin, emptiness, and trauma. The consistent bat swings of life never stop, but hit differently as we grow and mature in Christ. He softens the blows and we persevere more graciously every time. Our souls are refreshed by Him and He is renewing us day by day.

I might have a bit of a chip on my shoulder about certain things. I'm working on it. I've uncovered a lot and recovered from those things that were caused by trauma – within and outside of family. There is always work to do as long as I'm human. I hope the Lord never stops working on me, and that my heart stays malleable and aware of my shortcomings so that my sails veer towards Him. I hope I can look up at the end of my life with a big smile and say, "there is wonderful joy ahead!" (1 Peter 1:6). Because with God, I know it's only gotten better with time, that it will continue to, and that this life isn't all there is. Eternity with my King is ahead and with Him, I know it gets better. And better, and better, and better.

Scriptures about sex

Drink water from your own well—share your love only with your wife. Why spill the water of your springs in the streets, having sex with just anyone? You should reserve it for yourselves. Never share it with strangers. Proverbs 5:15-17

But because of the temptation for sexual immorality, each man should have his own wife, and each woman her own husband. 1 Corinthians 7:2

The husband should give to his wife her conjugal rights, and likewise the wife to her husband. 4 For the wife does not have authority over her own body, but the husband does. Likewise the husband does not have authority over his own body, but the wife does. 1 Corinthians 7: 3-4

Do not deprive each other of sexual relations unless you both agree to refrain from sexual intimacy for a limited time so you can give yourselves more completely to prayer. Afterward, you should come together again so that Satan won't be able to tempt you because of your lack of self-control. 1 Corinthians 7:5

Run from sexual sin! No other sin so clearly affects the body as this one does. For sexual immorality is a sin against your own body. Don't you realize that your body is the temple of the Holy Spirit, who lives in you and was given to you by God? You do not belong to yourself, for God bought you with a high price. So, you must honor God with your body. 1 Corinthians 6:18-20

God's will is for you to be holy, so stay away from all sexual sin. Then each of you will control his own body and live in holiness and honor— not in lustful passion like the pagans who do not know God and his ways" 1 Thessalonians 4:3-4

Marriage should be honored by all, and the marriage bed kept pure, for God will judge the adulterer and all the sexually immoral. Hebrews 13:4

Everyone who looks at a woman with lustful intent has already committed adultery with her in his heart. Matthew 5:28

Those who indulge in sexual sin, or commit adultery, or are male prostitutes, or practice homosexuality, none of these will inherit the Kingdom of God. 1 Corinthians 6:9

Should a man take his body, which is part of Christ, and join it to a prostitute? Never! And don't you realize that if a man joins himself to a prostitute, he becomes one body with her? For the Scriptures say, 'The two are united into one. 1 Corinthians 6:16

In the same way, husbands ought to love their wives as they love their own bodies. For a man who loves his wife actually shows love for himself. Ephesians 5:28

May your fountain be blessed, and may you rejoice in the wife of your youth. A loving doe, a graceful deer— may her breasts satisfy you always, may you ever be intoxicated with her love. Proverbs 5:18-19

As the Scriptures say, 'A man leaves his father and mother and is joined to his wife, and the two are united into one.' This is a great mystery, but it is an illustration of the way Christ and the church are one. Ephesians 5:31-32

These are just a handful of amazing guidance on how we're to live in the parameters of our sexuality. I also highly recommend reading Song of Solomon, it beautifully (and in detail!) shows the intimacy God intended for there to be within a marriage. I also love these quotes that wisely sum up the connection of the conventional union between two people and the Lord:

"The free exchange of consent properly witnessed by the Church establishes the marriage bond. Sexual union consummates it – seals it, completes it, perfects it. Sexual union, then, is where the words of the wedding vows become flesh." Christopher West

"The monstrosity of sexual intercourse outside marriage is that those who indulge in it are trying to isolate one kind of union (the sexual) from all the other kinds of union which were intended to go along with it and make up the total union." C. S. Lewis

Prayer to know Jesus and surrender your life to Him:

Father in the name of Jesus, please forgive me for my sins and who I've been. I want to know you, I want to invite you into my heart and make your home within me. Please create a clean heart in me God and place your Holy Spirit in my heart. I want to walk with you daily and fight the good fight of faith. I want to see your hand in everything, and be more like you. Make me a new creation in you! I surrender everything in my life to you. Thankyou for diy g on the cross for me and giving me the gift of eternal life! In Jesus' name, Amen!

Yay! Congratulations to you and welcome to the fam. If you've just prayed this, you made the best decision you've ever made in your entire life. Go seek Him in His word and talk with Him to get to know His character, so that you can develop a deeper relationship with Him!

Whoever calls on the name of the Lord shall be saved. (Romans 10:13)

Therefore, if anyone is in Christ, the new creation has come: The old has gone, the new is here! (2 Corinthians 5:17)

For God so loved the world that he gave his one and only Son, that whoever believes in him shall not perish but have eternal life. (John 3:16

www.ingramcontent.com/pod-product-compliance
Lightning Source LLC
Chambersburg PA
CBHW060518080526
44586CB00012B/529